# Praise fɤ

"*In* NOW WHAT?, *Jennifer Fondrevay has created an indispensable handbook for anyone navigating corporate change. She writes from experience with compassion, wit, and insight. The book is equal parts humor (think* The Office*), drama (think* Game of Thrones*), and inspiration (think* Eat, Pray, Love*). If you are facing the emotional and political tsunami of a corporate change, whether M&A, restructuring or transformation,* NOW WHAT? *is your lifeboat to get your bearings, stay afloat and make it to shore with your job, dignity, and sanity intact.*"
    —Mark Bonchek, PhD, CEO (Chief Epiphany Officer),
    Shift Thinking

"*Jennifer Fondrevay maps out the treacherous road of M&A integration! She walks you down the risky back alleys and dead-end streets of the journey, coaching you on what to expect, why those things happen, plus how best to manage yourself and your career through the process. Her focus is on the people side of integration—the place where most mergers go bad—and she holds your interest with her fresh perspective, satire, and humor. She does a great job of putting you in touch with yourself, the situation, and how to make the most of it. This is a book for people caught in the middle of M&A: the vulnerable middle managers and the many rank-and-file who are at the mercy of the dealmakers. Those execs have their playbook.* NOW WHAT? *is the playbook for "everyman."*"
    —Price Pritchett, PhD, M&A Thought Leader and
    Best Selling Author of *Lessons from 1,000 deals*

"With mergers and acquisitions one of the go-to levers in corporation's growth toolkits, the need to get them right is more acute than ever. Unfortunately, most still tank miserably, leaving massive destruction and waste in their wake. Jennifer Fondrevay has translated her decades of in-the-M&A-trenches experience into a battle tested, entertaining, and sometimes disturbingly honest guidebook to help you beat the painful odds stacked against you. Don't be another statistic as you enter your M&A whitewater. Just follow the wisdom on the pages ahead."

—Ron Carucci, Managing Partner at Navalent;
Best Selling Author of *Rising to Power:
The Journey of Exceptional Executives*

"Through a series of real-life stories and her own experience, Jennifer Fondrevay created an 'M&A survival guide' for every person going through an M&A experience. Her examples are relatable, and her advice is practical and to-the-point. Whether you are on the acquirer or acquired side of the deal, this is a must-read for anybody going through an acquisition. Thumbs-up!"

—Ana Dutra, Global Corporate Board Director;
Speaker, Best Selling Author of
*Lessons in Leadershit: Detoxing the Workplace*

"Middle managers and front-line leaders often feel stranded when going through the upheaval of a merger. Jennifer Fondrevay shares practical, easy to apply strategies to help your leaders thrive before, during and after your organization grows through a merger or acquisition."

—Greg Schinkel, President, Front Line Leadership
Systems; Author of *What Great Supervisors Know*

"The letters "M" and "A" can bring panic to the people whose lives will be impacted by a potential merger. First things first: DON'T PANIC! Next up, READ THIS BOOK! Jennifer's decades-long experience with mergers and acquisitions provides the necessary tools to guide people through the perfect roadmap to follow to not just survive the process, but thrive. Change can be scary, but in this day and age it's adapt, change, or die."

—Jeffrey Hayzlett, Primetime TV & Podcast Host,
Speaker, Author and Part-Time Cowboy

"An M&A wreaks havoc on the emotional operating system of the people in your organization. With all the moving parts of an M&A, your most precious resource—your employees—are in fight and flight mode. Jennifer Fondrevay writes the M&A survival manual with surprising humor after 3 major M&A experiences. I encourage you to read NOW WHAT? to understand all the short-cuts to understanding the different personality types you will encounter so you're not sabotaged from the very start."

—Caroline Stokes, CEO, FORWARD;
Author of Elephants Before Unicorns: Emotionally
Intelligent HR Strategies to Save Your Company

"Fondrevay's book should be the go-to source for anyone involved on either side of an M&A deal. With NOW WHAT? she captures the practical and tactical actions which, if taken, will drive success or if not, will increase frustration and likely failure. It begins with attitude. She emphatically points out that if you expect the resulting environment to be better than expected or worse than expected, it will be. Just because the majority of mergers fail, you as an individual do not have to suffer the same consequences. If you find yourself in the middle of an M&A deal transaction, pick up a copy of this very readable book!"

—William J White, Former Chairman/CEO of Bell & Howell
Co; Northwestern Professor and Author of From Day One

"*Jennifer Fondrevay's,* NOW WHAT? *is what has been missing from the M&A playbook for decades, but no longer. The millions of workers and executives who are destined to go through mergers and acquisitions have a new tool: this book. Having been a corporate director who went through a major merger, I wish I had then a resource to counsel employees and colleagues. We do now, and* NOW WHAT? *provides the roadmap to getting through the perils and unknowns of a merger, and especially, how to survive.*"

—Peter Tanous, Chairman, Lynx Investment Advisory, Washington DC; Best Selling Author of *Investment Gurus*

"*Jennifer Fondrevay's book provides a wonderful opportunity to honestly reflect on what makes the complex world of M&A either a success or failure. For companies who acquire businesses, too often the focus is on valuations, deal models, or the desire to be acquisitive, but* NOW WHAT? *is a pointed reminder of the real key to successful M&A: people. Jennifer's writing encapsulates many realities of human psychology from both the perspective of the acquiring and the acquired, and offers practical and entertaining perspectives and advice on the opportunities, challenges, and watch-outs. This book is a must-read for leaders of all levels on both sides of M&A deals to maximize the opportunities for successful integration and value creation.*"

—Joel Grade, EVP and Chief Financial Officer, Sysco

# Other Business Books by Cortado Press

*The Worst Business Model in the World:*
*A New Kind of Guide for a New Kind of Entrepreneur*
by Danny Schuman

# NOW WHAT?

# A Survivor's Guide for Thriving through Mergers and Acquisitions

By Jennifer J. Fondrevay

Cover design by Jess Hanebury

Book design by Alex Head / Draft Lab

Illustrations by Jeff York

Editorial assistance by Amelia Forczak at pithywordsmithery.com

Library of Congress Control Number: 2019915738

ISBN: 978-1-7341113-0-9

Printed in the United States of America

*To Pops, Abuelita and Smushie for being my original supporters.*

*To Greg, Yvonne and Connor for letting
their belief in my idea never waiver.*

# Table of Contents

## Section 1—Why Mergers and Acquisitions Occur: The People Consequences

## Section 2—The M&A Stages of Grief

# Section 3—The Post-M&A Cast of Characters

# Section 4—Now What?

# FOREWORD

## By Dorie Clark

Executive Education faculty,
Duke University Fuqua School of Business
Author of *Reinventing You*, *Stand Out*
*Entrepreneurial You*

Almost on a daily basis, we read about business seg-ments or industries being disrupted or transformed, with multibillion-dollar companies and smaller organiza-tions alike experiencing mergers and acquisitions (M&A) on a regular basis. And despite their poor success rate, M&A deals continue to be a popular growth strategy as businesses globally struggle to survive. It's safe to say that mergers or acquisitions affect millions of people, and given the lack of preparedness that occurs with dramatic change, not in a good way.

Jennifer Fondrevay should know. She's the survivor of three multibillion-dollar acquisitions. I got to know Jen-nifer when she joined my community of Recognized Ex-perts, a course rooted in the principles of my best-selling business book *Stand Out.* As an internationally experienced Fortune 500 executive, Jennifer witnessed the downside of mergers and acquisitions and saw an opportunity to improve their success rate—by focusing on the people most affected.

Jennifer has been on both sides of the equation—acquirer and acquiree. Along with this experienced perspective, she brings a fire and passion that comes through in her insightful advice and guidance. Most people center on the deal making and what needs to be done to make the deal happen. They rarely focus on what ultimately makes the deal a success or failure: the people.

Jennifer shines a spotlight on the people part of M&A, focusing on why M&A deals are pursued, who will bear the brunt of the deal's expectations, and how they can manage through it for success. She provides a survivor's frame of reference, focused on addressing managers' needs and concerns while showing executives the people challenges they can expect.

Business transformation is tough enough, and M&A deals bring unique emotional challenges that compound the difficulty for managers. The organizational challenges are well documented, but there's also a personal dimension, as managers grapple with their own evolving emotions while also trying to understand their colleagues' or subordinates' shifting behaviors. People can get lost in the shuffle or lose their way. This focus on the emotional challenges of M&A is part of what makes *NOW WHAT?* such a valuable resource.

A practical guide for the people in the middle of the storm is what has been lacking—until now. With a straightforward, "I-know-what-you're-going-through" tone and comical illustrations, *NOW WHAT?* delivers true-to-life insights into an M&A deal's roller coaster of emotions, guidance on how to work with new bosses and shifting colleagues, and a multi-step process on how to find career opportunity amidst the change and chaos. Whether you are an executive faced with leading a team post deal, or a manager trying to make sense of it all, *NOW WHAT?* is the manual you need to succeed.

# PREFACE

We don't know each other yet, but I want to be straight up with you—I wrote this book for you. How do I know this book is for you? Because this is the book I wish I'd had when I was going through my acquisition experiences. Particularly the first one.

In the early 2000s, I worked at NAVTEQ, a technology company that was making a digital map of every road and walkway in the world. I loved that company and the people. I poured my heart and soul into it. I even dragged my husband and two small kids to France to lead B2B marketing across Europe, the Middle East, Africa, and Russia. Back then, if you'd asked me to describe my dream job, this was it.

Then in 2008, NAVTEQ was acquired by Nokia. It made complete sense. Nokia was all about connecting people, and our maps and expertise would help them do that.

Let's just say the $8.8 billion acquisition didn't quite live up to expectations. It was an experience I'll never forget. But going into the specific details of the NAVTEQ acquisition is not the point of this book. The point of this book is to share what I learned from that experience, and the two subsequent acquisitions I endured, so you can better prepare for your own M&A journey.

Since then, I've interviewed more than 60 people who have all been through a merger or acquisition. I interviewed company owners, senior executives, middle managers, private equity folks, and everyone in between. The interviewees worked for companies that were acquired and companies that did the acquiring. Some were serial acquirers who had been through M&A over and over and over. They each shared their experiences and hard-fought lessons learned to help me create this survivor's handbook.

In the interviews, what I heard repeatedly was how much companies and their employees needed the insights and guidance that my book provided. That too often deals failed because of "unexpected people problems."

I founded my M&A consultancy, Day1 Ready™, because the same people issues I experienced continue to come up time after time after time. When my *Harvard Business Review* article, "After the Merger, Don't let Us vs. Them Thinking Ruin the Company,"[1] went viral, it confirmed there was a growing interest in a more human-centric approach to business transformation, with employees at the heart of the change, not on the sidelines. I've dedicated my future to giving a voice to this more human-centric approach to M&A. I work with companies, from Fortune 500, to small and midsized businesses (SMB), to entrepreneurial start-ups to help people not only survive M&A, but to thrive in it.

Throughout my experience, I've found that no matter how scary M&A seems, in the endearing words of Monty Python, "Always look on the bright side of life." There is upside to be found. You just have to look for it. In M&A, having a positive attitude can lead to opportunity.

One of my goals in writing this book is to prevent you from being blindsided if and when your company goes through M&A. And with M&A deals on the rise, the likelihood you will experience it increases daily. This guide will help you navigate the chaos and your emotions to recognize how M&A can in fact further your career, teaching you how to play your cards right and capitalize on the opportunities. We're in this together.

# INTRODUCTION

Let's be honest. The mere mention of a merger or acquisition might be enough to send your emotions into a tailspin. No one can prepare you for the emotional rollercoaster ride of an M&A deal. When faced with unexpected change, it's hard not to imagine the worst: the fear of fighting a losing battle to show your worth and keep your job, the dread of reporting to tyrannical new leaders, the anxiety of going from a pleasant work environment to a hellish one. If you harbor these dark thoughts about mergers and acquisitions, know that you are not alone. After all, there have been enough nightmare-inducing M&A tales out there to make it seem like doom and gloom are the only things to expect.

But no matter how scary M&A seems, having a positive attitude can lead to opportunity. This book will help you navigate the chaos so you can recognize how M&A can help your career. If you are prepared to manage the many stresses involved, you will be better able to recognize and capitalize on the numerous opportunities available to you.

Before we go any further, let's make sure we're on the same page with some key terms:

- **M&A** is the general term for deals involving the buying, selling, and combining of companies and business entities via two forms of business combinations—merger (M) and acquisition (A). Sometimes you see the terms used interchangeably, as if they are one and the same. While they are both business amalgamation approaches (well that's a mouthful!), they are markedly different in execution.

- A **merger** is when two companies join together to form a new company. An example would be the DaimlerChrysler Company, which was formed when two originally separate companies—Daimler-Benz and Chrysler—agreed to move forward as a single, united company (at least they were united at first).

- In an **acquisition**, one company is purchased by another company. Unlike a merger, no new company is formed. The purchasing company simply absorbs the other. For example, when Amazon acquired Whole Foods in 2017, they did not become Amazon-Whole Foods, but you did start to see changes at Whole Foods influenced by Amazon.

For our purposes, M&A is any kind of transaction where majority ownership of a company changes hands. It could be a bigger company buying a smaller company, a private equity firm building a multi-billion-dollar portfolio of companies, or an individual owner retiring and selling the business she built. All of these situations create changes in leadership. The person who was calling the shots is no longer in charge, and that means absolutely anything can change—anything—even things that always seemed central to the company's identity and success.

M&A happens for a variety of complex reasons, but in my experience, it boils down to two general factors:

- **Growth:** All companies are in the business of making money, and sometimes it makes financial sense to join with other companies in the hopes of becoming even more profitable. There are many ways that growth can kickstart profitability, and M&A deals often transpire to create combination opportunities.

- **Succession planning:** When company owners don't want to be owners anymore, and a significant portion of their wealth is the value of the company, they need to sell their portion of the company to move on and cash out.

We'll get into more detail later, but for now, the important point is that companies are increasingly pursuing M&A as a growth strategy as it becomes a viable way to keep from going out of business.

And yet, while M&A can be a viable solution for the overall good of a company, it's extremely difficult from a people perspective. A deal can be perfect on paper but not work in real life because of how people react to change.

According to HBR and McKinsey studies, 70–90% of M&A deals fail to achieve their objectives within the designated timeframe.[2] The most often cited reason? "Unexpected people problems."[3] In other words, people are the wild card.

We have emotions that aren't always logical, with fears and egos that can take over our behavior, clouding common sense and inhibiting our ability to make practical decisions. Above all else, as creatures of habit, we abhor change. So, it's not surprising that we are the reason so many M&A deals go south.

I'm not blaming employees; I blame human psychology. As much as people love winning, we are even more motivated to avoid losing. Think about it—if you found $50 on the street, you would be happy. But how would that level of emotion compare to losing $50? Chances are you would spend a lot more time lamenting all the things you could have purchased with that $50 (A tank of gas! At least eight lattes! A nice bottle of wine!) than enjoying what an extra $50 would buy you. In cognitive psychology, this is called loss aversion.[4] Some studies suggest that, psychologically, losses are twice as powerful as gains.[5] Chalk it up to survival instincts, but we really don't like to lose what we have.

The reality of M&A is that due to the nature of change, many of the old ways of doing things will go away. Some losses might seem minor but feel major, like the annual company picnic, a familiar health insurance plan, or your number of vacation days. Other potential losses will be major and feel catastrophic, like losing certain job responsibilities, a demotion in title or social standing within the company, or loss of autonomy. (And that's just what you might experience if you keep your job!)

When faced with this level of change, people start to act a little crazy. I can confirm from personal experience that unpredictable emotions can rage when people are operating from a position of fear. Fight or flight kicks in and the claws come out. Self-preservation comes above all else when people are afraid for their job, their livelihood. The things that once made a company and its people successful—teamwork, communication, and a customer-centric focus—can be turned upside down. Yet it doesn't need to be that way.

To prevent this tailspin, it's essential to understand what you can expect through an M&A deal so you can instead focus on the opportunities that arise. A merger or acquisition can provide new work and responsibilities that better align with your passions and interests. But to capitalize on these opportunities, you have to be open to them.

## How to use this book

This book includes four sections designed to help guide you through the process of M&A. The first deals with the question, "Why is this happening?" I believe that the more context you have for why M&A happens, the more prepared you will be when it does. By understanding the drivers behind M&A and the top reasons they fail, you can anticipate what's coming, mitigate the risks, and start to appreciate where the opportunities might be.

The second section reveals the post-deal experience for what it is: a journey from denial to acceptance through the M&A stages of grief. Everybody, and I do mean everybody, experiences this progression in some way. It doesn't matter if you merged, were acquired, or acquired another. There's always a sense of loss for the way things were.

In the third section, I introduce the cast of characters who emerge post deal. From the Former Rock Star to the Know-Nothing, you will discover the personalities that M&A tend to bring out—and that includes former co-workers. Beyond identifying the personalities, this section provides tips and suggestions on how to work with them, whether they are your boss or a new teammate. You will also learn how to manage your actions and behaviors if you find yourself becoming one of the characters in this book.

The final section will combine what we've learned to help you construct a total "survive and thrive" game plan. The clearer you are on the mission and vision of your company, and where you fit within that mission, the clearer your path forward becomes. And when you know your true value within this new equation, you can position yourself to create new opportunities, at your company or elsewhere.

If you sense M&A on the horizon, this book will help prepare you for what's to come, providing the tools you'll need to guide yourself through this trying time. M&A is a progression, and the structure of this book follows this process through each step. Perhaps you already find yourself in the midst of a deal and are looking for answers to the chaos around you. This book is for you too. Read what feels beneficial, and read this in the order you wish. Just like the M&A journey, this book doesn't need to be read in a linear fashion. But know that understanding the roots of what you're experiencing (particularly the stages of M&A grief) is key to moving forward.

Above all else—know that you will get through this. This emotional journey can sometimes drag you through the low trough of despair. But with this handbook at your side, you will have a better idea of what to expect, enabling you to recognize the opportunities before you. Once you see those opportunities, a whole new world will open up.

You got this.

# SECTION
# 1

Why Mergers and
Acquisitions Occur: The
People Consequences

# CHAPTER 1

# Market Forces That Drive M&A

Dealing with M&A might feel like a result of the times; that we're all just lucky enough to be of working age at a time when the rate of M&A deals has never been higher. But M&A, the concept of merging or acquiring for growth, isn't about a particular decade, or even a particular century. M&A has been going on for as long as people have been on this planet. Seriously. Some of the first M&A deals go back to feudal times. Although they did not use the same fancy corporate jargon, rulers back then were essentially pursuing the same goals through conquest and domination.

Think about it: Vikings and Romans integrated tribes; the Mongols wiped out their competition through conquest; Columbus "discovered" America, acquiring "new" land and resources for the Spanish. The British Empire acquired colonies and land all over the globe, at one point ruling more than 23 percent of the world population.[6] It seems that power has always had a way of growing through mergers or acquisitions.

For kings, growing the kingdom was practically the only

duty that mattered. They acquired land through conquering other kingdoms or marrying into it. Hell, the French even have a saying, *"le choix du Roi"* (the King's choice), which today translates as "congrats, you had a boy and now a girl, what luck for you," but which back then meant, "Congratulations King, you have your choice in conquest since the son can take the throne and the daughter can be married to another kingdom's prince" (read: even bigger opportunities for more land and power!).

While the dominating entities have changed over the centuries, you get the picture—ruling over land and resources was the *path to power,* and leaders either did it by *acquisition of* or *merger with* other tribes, countries, etc.

In the 21st century, mergers and acquisitions create power shifts every day, all over the world. Thankfully, it's no longer happening through brute force, but sometimes it can feel just as scary.

Sometimes employees see it coming (lots of guys in blue suits and briefcases, hanging out in your conference room), sometimes they know something is up but aren't sure what is going on, and other times they are blindsided by it. If you don't have a clue that change is on the horizon, it can make the whole situation tougher. But even if you know something's up, it can still be a shock when you learn you've been acquired.

If you are in the middle of M&A deal dynamics, all you care about is how to get through it. I understand completely, and I'm here to help you navigate this "new normal." But first, we need to understand why your company pursued an M&A deal in the first place. Knowing this will better prepare you for what's to come.

As we all know, companies need to grow their business in order to succeed. Changing market dynamics can make it easier or tougher to do this. When these market circumstances occur, and especially when two or more combine, we see a serious uptick in the number of mergers and acquisitions. That's why M&A activity typically comes in waves.

In the last 130 years, there have been six waves of merger activity in the U.S. We are currently experiencing the seventh. By examining the market forces that made M&A appealing in the past, you'll be in better shape to understand whether your company might be considering M&A as a growth strategy.

- **Wave 1: The Great Merger Movement—1890–1910** Horizontal mergers, often from rivals in the same industry, began uniting companies to form monopolies. The industries that most quickly turned into monopolies were steel, oil, railroads, telephone, and mining. These kinds of M&A deals were later deemed by the government to be harmful to the economy, so legislation was passed to prevent "anti-competitive behavior" in business.

- **Wave 2: The Vertical Merger Wave—1919–1929** Since companies could no longer form industry monopolies, they went vertical instead, combining companies that collaborated in the supply chain. The auto industry was a key player in this wave, acquiring companies that produced materials needed in the manufacturing process. Vertical mergers ultimately reduced costs and increased efficiencies for companies by streamlining production. This wave ended when the stock market crashed, and the Great Depression began.

- **Wave 3: The Conglomerate Wave—1955–1970** Companies wanted to expand, but they had to move beyond horizontal and vertical mergers to find more opportunities for growth. Businesses that had virtually nothing to do with one another began merging, forming larger organizations with diversified offerings. General Electric, which had businesses ranging from manufacturing equipment to television and even financial services, is a good example of this. Diversifying is great for companies because it helps them hedge risk. With eggs in multiple baskets, it's easier for companies to be strategic about where to allocate resources and focus even more growth. And if one business line isn't doing well, it won't sink the whole company.

- **Wave 4: The Deregulation Wave—Late 1970s–1990** Government regulations play a big role in enabling or prohibiting M&A, and in the '70s, the U.S. government started relaxing anti-merger and merger-control legislation that had been in place since the monopoly debacle of the first M&A wave. Additionally, many sectors of business were deregulated, making M&A possible for a broader range of companies. In those conditions, all a company needed was enough money to make the purchase. Lucky for them, interest rates were low, and investment banks were lending lots of money. This wave became marked by "hostile takeovers," in which a large corporation or investor would buy enough of another company to simply take control of it—whether or not there were obvious synergies between companies. When the market crashed in 1987, this wave soon came to an end.

- **Wave 5: The Mega-Merger Wave—1993-2000**
  This is the first wave where international companies became a major part of the M&A action, thanks in large part to more deregulation. This wave was also driven by creating economies of scale, meaning that the more you make of something, the cheaper it is to produce. With international companies merging, opportunities to drive down operating costs and production costs in the supply chain increased. Wave 5 created some of the largest companies in the world today, in industries ranging from pharmaceuticals, to oil, to banking, and telecommunications.

- **Wave 6: The Shareholder Wave—2003-2008**
  Interest rates dipped to their lowest point in decades, so it was good timing for companies to borrow money to acquire other companies in hopes of making even more money. Private equity firms also became more involved in M&A. In the early 2000s, shareholders of publicly traded companies also became more vocal in influencing company decisions. Shareholders care deeply about the price

of stocks, and they put pressure on company leaders to make decisions that would boost their value. Their viewpoints began playing a major factor in many companies' M&A decisions. This wave came to a screeching halt when the U.S. housing market tanked the economy at home and abroad.[7,8]

That brings us to the current wave of M&A: **The Digital Wave**. Perhaps better described as a tsunami, it is the biggest yet, largely driven by high rates of innovation, technological advancement, and globalization. Just consider the fact that in 2015, M&A activity hit its all-time high, reaching $5 trillion in deals completed.

$5,000,000,000,000. Take that in. Twelve zeros!

Maybe you heard about, or were personally affected by some of the biggest mergers and acquisitions of the seventh wave:

- Dow Chemical acquired DuPont for $130 billion (2015)
- Anheuser-Busch InBev acquired SAB Miller for $107 billion (2015)
- Heinz acquired Kraft for $100 billion (2015)
- AT&T acquired Time Warner for $86 billion (2018)
- Bristol-Myers Squib acquired Celgene for $74 billion (2019)
- The Walt Disney Company acquired 21st Century Fox for $71 billion (2019)[9]

These are only a few of the big M&A deals in this wave. Looking at this handful of acquisitions and the astronomical amounts of money changing hands, it feels almost strange, unreal. The billions of dollars have an aura of play money tossed in handfuls across a Monopoly board. And yet hundreds of thousands of individuals' lives are affected.

## Current market forces

Just like the previous six waves, the current wave is driven by a few market forces:

- **Technology:** Sometimes referred to as the "digital deal," large companies often pursue M&A with the purpose of acquiring new technologies. They seek a "digital transformation" of their current operations. Having a strong digital component can help a company grow faster. According to *Harvard Business Review*, "more than half of U.S. companies logging M&A activity described themselves as primarily acquiring digital companies or assets ... The disruption and differentiation that digital technology can create will place it at the center of acquisition strategy for the foreseeable future."[10] Technology has changed every industry, from refrigerators that tell you when you need to buy more eggs, to your doctor's office texting you appointment reminders. Improving the technology component of just about any business is a win, and as technology continues to advance exponentially, it will keep driving the M&A activity you see today.

- **Scale:** Although scale has been a driving market force for M&A in past waves, it is becoming a greater opportunity across many more industries. Leveraging technology, businesses are able to grow more quickly via M&A deals than they have in the past. This is true even when companies merge to provide a broad array of products or services that span multiple industries. Companies get the benefit of add-on growth strategies while also unlocking opportunities for improving companywide operational efficiencies. Post M&A deal, these newly formed companies are often able to keep providing the exact same things, but they do so with fewer people and resources. That's how positions—and even entire departments—are deemed redundant, leading to lay-offs. On the flip side, growing companies also create new, *different* jobs. For example, you see mom-and-pop businesses disappearing, but companies like Amazon are hiring scores of people to work in warehouses, do your grocery shopping, and deliver your purchases right to your front door.

- **Globalization:** When you feel like you've sold as much as you can to your local market, a great option to sell more is to expand to other markets. But starting out as an unknown entity in a new location is hard, especially when expanding across borders or oceans. It's much easier to partner with another company that is well-established. They already have employees who know the language and market, and they have existing distribution, sales, etc. This is why companies often pursue M&A when they want to increase their global footprint. Combined with enhanced technology and easier scalability, expanding into new markets has fewer barriers than it once did, so we see more and more companies taking advantage of the opportunity.

With these powerful market forces combining, the rate of mergers and acquisitions is expected to increase for the foreseeable future. As more and more companies merge to get a leg up on their competition, it's making it even harder for others to thrive when they choose to go it alone. That's why this M&A wave feels like a cycle in which the momentum keeps building. It's transcending industries, rapidly changing global brands, and affecting the employment of hundreds of thousands of workers.

Understanding these market forces will give you the advantage of seeing M&A on the horizon instead of being blindsided by it. Your insight may also help you better appreciate the advantages that M&A brings to companies—even when change seems like an uphill battle.

# CHAPTER 2

# Understanding the Signs of M&A at Your Company

Now that you understand the driving forces in the economy that contribute to M&A, it might seem like M&A can happen to anyone, anywhere, at any time. It's true M&A is prevalent these days, but in certain circumstances it becomes much more likely individual companies will consider it. The good news is that you don't need a crystal ball to know if M&A is on the horizon. By staying informed on industry trends while keeping an eye out for certain scenarios playing out at work, you'll have an advantage for spotting an M&A deal's potential, often long before any deals are made. This insight will enable you to emotionally prepare while figuring out how to add value if your company pivots directions.

## Declining revenue

When your company routinely falls short of projected revenue goals, it is a pretty good sign that trouble is brewing. Something needs to change. There are a lot of reasons for declining revenue, but the key point is that companies often address this challenge by considering an M&A deal. (And there might come a time when that's the only solution besides closing company doors.) M&A can be the boost needed for a business to survive, whether it's getting the funding to develop a game-changing product line or bringing in new talent to help the company readjust priorities. When companies merge, they often do so to lower operating costs by eliminating redundancies. For this reason, a company that has declining revenue could be an attractive acquisition target, especially if it comes at a bargain price.

So, how do you know if your company's revenue is declining? Publicly traded companies share earnings on a quarterly basis, so it's easy for employees to stay in the know. Privately owned companies aren't always as transparent: Some owners choose to share revenue information in all-company meetings, whereas others keep employees on a need-to-know basis. Even if you haven't heard directly from the horse's mouth, there are a lot of ways to tell if revenue is declining:

- You lose a couple big contracts or a lot of little contracts
- The sales team always seems to miss their goals (At first, this might have looked like a talent issue, but now it looks like something else.)
- Raises and bonuses are smaller than expected or non-existent
- You aren't hiring for new positions and haven't in a while

- The office is starting to look shabby, and equipment is dated
- People have been told to cut back on company travel
- Smaller expenses go through a more in-depth approval process than they once did
- It's been a long time since your company celebrated good news

Not all of these signs are sure ways to tell if your company is losing money, but when combined—especially over an extended period—there's a good chance the business leaders or owners are at least considering a merger or an acquisition with another company.

## Succession planning

Just about all business owners want to retire or move on at some point, and for small and mid-sized companies, this means ownership has to change hands. For companies with a sole owner, it can be difficult to find a person who has enough cash to buy the business. Often, those who have the money (and interest) to buy the business already own other businesses, so getting a new owner may require an M&A deal. In a company with multiple owners, it's possible for the owners to "buy out" the person who wants to leave, but this can be prohibitively expensive or worse, put former partners at odds. It takes liquidity—cash—to buy someone out. And the more successful the business, the more it's going to cost. So, when one owner wants to sell, a reasonable option might be joining forces with another company or a private equity firm.

In family owned businesses, all of this gets much more emotionally charged. Most often, business owners have poured their lives into building up their companies; the business is in their blood. But that feeling isn't always shared by family members. Sometimes owners don't think family members are capable of running the business, and other times no one in the family shows interest, so selling to a third-party may be the only solution the owner believes will keep the business afloat.

Succession planning can be difficult for small businesses. So much energy is put into the day-to-day that it's hard to stop and think about the future. Equally tough is that small businesses become like family as employees develop personal relationships with the owners, so it can be difficult for owners to let go. While there is usually some sense of when owners might want to leave, given their age, family commitments, and general passion for the work, it can take years longer than employees might expect. When there isn't a clear succession plan, it's a possible sign that an M&A deal will be considered.

## Critical gaps in products, resources, or talent for long-term success

As customer preferences and technology evolve, companies often discover gaps in their ability to meet changing demand. For example, let's say you work for a successful lightbulb company that sells one kind of bulb. Lately, customers have been asking for another kind of bulb. You're still doing okay, but as demand for this other lightbulb grows, you start to lose business. With this shift in the market, your company needs to find a way to start making the kind of bulb customers are requesting or partner with a company that's already selling it. The longer it takes to bring this product to market, the more market share you'll lose. With this in mind, you can see how the "easy button" is often to acquire a company that makes the desired product to immediately fill the gap.

As another example, your company might have a gap in talent. Perhaps your company could use an engineering team to develop better products, a sales and marketing team that could connect with a new target market, or senior leaders that have the vision needed to pivot and grow. When your business could benefit from bringing on new people, an M&A could (or should) be on the horizon.

This M&A driver can be a little harder to predict depending on your vantage point in the company. Some roles are impacted by gaps, while others are largely unaffected. To make it even more complicated, some gaps creep in over time, whereas others become an emergency practically overnight. To better notice and predict these gaps, focus on the future. What (or who) could make your company better? The answer might be the reason your company pursues M&A.

## Innovation or disruption in your industry

As competitors evolve their offerings, it redefines what customers think about your company's offerings. Your company might need to adjust to meet changing expectations and stay relevant. One way to do that is through M&A.

For example, Unilever was selling plenty of ice cream through brands Breyer's and Good Humor, but who wants chocolate ice cream when they could have Chunky Monkey? Ben & Jerry's made people crave unique flavors, so Unilever found itself under pressure. They could have come up with new flavors or new branding and marketing to make those flavors seem cool, but it was ultimately easier to acquire Ben & Jerry's. (Ironically, Unilever announced this acquisition the same day they announced their plans to acquire Slim-Fast. Go figure.)[11]

Here are a few indicators that your industry is ripe for disruption (or that you're already being disrupted):

- A change in consumer tastes (away from what you deliver)
- A transformation in customer expectations via advanced technology, enhanced services, or improved conveniences
- New innovations that better serve target markets or even create new ones

Your company can be on either side of this disruption. If the changing industry landscape is a threat to your business, your company might pursue M&A as a solution. If your company is growing and getting more and more business, you are eating into someone else's market share. This makes your company a possible acquisition target. This is true for businesses of any size.

Any up-and-coming business could eventually make an

industry-leader obsolete. Consider why Facebook bought Instagram for $1 billion in 2012. At the time of purchase, Instagram was not generating revenue. But after only two years, it had more than 30 million users, putting it on a trajectory to eat Facebook's lunch.[12] Instagram has recently been estimated to be worth $100 billion.

## Need for digital strategy/digital transformation

If your digital efforts, acquiring customers or serving them online, are lacking or non-existent, something needs to change. This is true in any industry. Amazon killed mom-and-pop bookstores, then they killed Borders Bookstores, a once-thriving national chain. Why did Barnes & Noble survive? Unlike Borders, they invested in online sales and developed their own digital e-reader, the Nook.[13] While they continue to struggle against Amazon, the fact is Barnes & Noble is still here. Having a tech component in a product or service offering can help attract customers, but it can also help behind the scenes by improving operations, optimizing processes, and bolstering efficiencies across the board. Walmart was hurt but not killed by Amazon because it transformed its digital strategy. A strong digital strategy can give companies the leg up needed to keep competition at bay.

To tell whether your company would benefit from a digital transformation, think in terms of challenges and opportunities. When a company has a particularly weak digital component, it's usually common knowledge to both employees and customers (e.g., everyone knows your competitor's interface is more user-friendly). Further opportunities for enhancing digital capabilities might be more easily seen by those serving specific job functions. What's holding your company back from reaching the next level? What could you do better if you had better technology or data? These are questions good company leaders think about every day. Sometimes the answers lead to M&A.

## Signs around the office

In addition to understanding the circumstances that could make your company ripe for M&A, there are signs around the office that can tip you off before it's announced. If you work for a small company, or you work closely with senior leaders, you have even more opportunities to spot change before any deals go down. That said, I want to make it clear that the point of this section is not to encourage your participation in the rumor mill! I simply want to give you the ability to process what you see and experience when your company explores M&A. Knowledge is power, as they say. Having this knowledge early will help you move through the M&A Stages of Grief, so that you can pivot and make yourself indispensable when priorities shift.

It's important to realize that owners, particularly SMB owners, tend to be incredibly private about considering M&A, since even speculation can damage customer relationships and future sales, as well as employee morale and productivity, resulting in the decline of a company's valuation. But even with clandestine M&A exploration, it's hard to keep the cat in the bag for long. Before owners make any decisions, they become subconsciously attuned to M&A-related information. They will hear and read things through that filter. Subsequently, their reactions and responses to topics or questions may shift as they interpret it through this new lens. I named my consultancy Day1 Ready™ based on this observation—day one is the day a business owner first considers a merger or an acquisition, because every decision after that is influenced by this frame of reference. You need to be ready for an M&A from that day forward because things have already changed by nature of having had the thought to pursue a deal.

Some leaders will eventually be brought into the know, but it will start with a limited number of highly trusted individuals. Even if none of these people spills the beans, attitudes and behaviors will begin to shift ever so slightly in different ways. A leader's decision-making or reactions to business topics (e.g., new products, digital efforts, new hiring) may prompt atypical responses. Astute managers will pick up on these shifts in attitude and decision making and recognize something's up.

M&A exploration becomes more visible in the office through mysterious meetings (where names are suspiciously missing from shared calendars or conference room schedules). Managers may get unusual requests for information, which is urgently needed by a seemingly arbitrary date or time. Senior executives are busier than usual and less available, but it's unclear how their time is being spent. This is usually followed by other unexplained changes, such as a reduced PR output or product and marketing efforts temporarily put on hold.

As suspicions increase, you may start to "compare notes." When not in earshot of the boss, people share what they see. A low hum of internal rumors begins. Competitors may eventually catch wind from leaks or loose lips. This is why even the most private mergers and acquisitions aren't always that private. Again, the key here is not to contribute to the rumor mill, but to stay smart and alert to shifts in attitude and behavior. It will prepare you for what's to come.

## Don't take it personally

The key thing to take away from this chapter is that a lot of thought and strategy go into a merger or acquisition. Contrary to what it might feel like, companies don't pursue M&A to ruin your life. Though you may feel blindsided by the news, leaders don't go into an M&A agreement lightly. Remember that leaders pursue M&A to keep the company solvent and growing. No matter how personal it feels, M&A is not about you. It is like musical chairs: when the music stops, sometimes you have a seat, sometimes you don't. It's not based on how fast or good you are; it's about where you are when the music stops. The arbitrariness might be enough to drive you insane, but hopefully it's enough to make you realize that you shouldn't take it personally.

Owners want their businesses to thrive, and you are one small part of a much, much larger decision. Unfortunately, M&A is disruptive by nature. Things tend to get worse before they get better. But in the midst of all the challenges and changes, there are opportunities. And you can capitalize on these opportunities to advance your career—you just have to get over the emotional hurdles that accompany these major changes. Which is where the next chapter comes in handy.

CHAPTER 3

# Minimize the Risk of Failure by Being Prepared

Now that you know M&A isn't about you (and trust me, it really isn't), it will be easier to emotionally distance yourself from what happens once the deal is done. As I've shared, statistics show that a high percentage of mergers and acquisitions do not go as smoothly as expected. So instead of just trying to stay calm and hoping for the best, understand what you're up against, prepare for whatever comes your way, and make your own opportunities.

When I first contemplated this book, I didn't want to base it on my experiences alone. It had to be a comprehensive survivor's handbook that included insights from other practitioners and survivors who had waded through the M&A jungle. I collected the experiences of executives and managers in companies large and small across a wide range of industries. More than 60 leaders shared their unique stories—good, bad, and ugly. I was surprised to hear the same issues mentioned over and over. The problems transpired in different ways, but they kept coming up, a trend reinforced by each new interview. I started feeling like a telepath. I could predict where the stories would go before my interviewees ever got to the juicy parts. One guy jokingly asked if I was a witch because I seemed to know a little too much.

Based on my research, I've identified the top three reasons mergers and acquisitions fail. It's critical for all professionals to be aware of these threats to M&A success—from the PE firms or executives at the top all the way to the newbies. By knowing what to watch out for, it's easier to prepare and confront issues before they become major problems that threaten your business.

## The top three reasons M&A deals fail

### Higher than anticipated complexity

Joining with another company can look simple on paper, but it rarely is. Every aspect of both businesses comes under scrutiny. From roles and responsibilities to systems, processes, and operations, the newly formed company needs to identify what's changing and what's not. Will both sides keep doing what they have been doing, will they switch to the other company's practices, or will they come up with an entirely new way of doing things? Often these questions are left to be figured out later, or the acquirer just assumes they will dictate the plan. Not considering these questions early on, however, can lead to significant issues later.

Part of the challenge occurs during the due diligence process because a limited number of people are aware of the deal in progress. Senior leaders may not appreciate the complexity of integrating processes, systems, and operations. (If you are one of these senior leaders, no offense!) Higher-ups, by nature of having moved up, are typically no longer involved in the day-to-day operations that make a business run smoothly. Furthermore, deal confidentiality requirements typically mean they can't consult the employees who actually *do* know. It's the equivalent of generals formulating battle plans without consulting their next in command. You know, the ones who have actual line of sight on the battlefield.

Though frustrating if you are a mid or lower-level manager, this can be a great opportunity for you to come in and inject the plan with much needed expertise. Those first 100 days are a critical time for frontline leaders to step up, identify challenges, and devise a plan to solve them. Identifying early on how to overcome issues paints you as a problem solver and positions you for a bigger role down the path. And that's what this is all about—positioning you as a key contributor.

## Difficult cultural fit

Let's be honest—this is where most of the drama occurs. Cultural differences can unravel the potential success of a deal in a short period of time, especially if those differences haven't been considered during negotiations. Company culture is typically pervasive amongst employees, and yet it is often hard to define. Add in global or regional differences, where timelines, responsiveness, and general communication can be totally different, and you see how quickly mismatched cultures can bring you down.

One interviewee told me about her Chicago-based company merging with an Orlando-based company. The Chicagoans quickly thought their southern coworkers were lazy and unreliable, while the southern employees thought the northerners were uptight and demanding. Indeed, company culture can be rooted in geography and perceived regional prejudices.

A critical aspect often overlooked is how a company defines its business priorities. Companies are typically either sales, product, or marketing driven. By prioritizing one of these as the driver of business, the company's philosophy grows around it. It becomes a core part of the company's identity, and employees are incentivized to bolster it. But when two businesses come together, priorities don't always align. For example, say a larger entity moves to acquire a small, innovative company because they have an attractive, potentially disruptive product. But the acquiring company's success is marketing-driven, and they don't place a lot of value on innovation. To ensure success, both companies need to value one another's priorities and see them as strengths that should be supported post-M&A deal. Unfortunately, that doesn't always happen.

Poor cultural fit was the most consistent challenge I heard during my interviews. A cultural misalignment can be devastating to M&A success due to tensions created among coworkers. Not valuing the way someone works can look and feel very similar to not valuing the person doing the work. And when colleagues don't value one another, communication shuts down.

To find success post deal, both companies need to come together and respect the other side. Look at it as you might the partnerships you most admire: each side clearly shows respect for the other. By valuing one another's priorities and way of doing business, you can find that common ground where the best of both companies comes together. Be humble and open to learning from the other side. That mindset allows you to create a stronger partnership.

## Synergies that did not materialize

When an M&A deal is planned, owners have high hopes for creating the perfect partnership. They see the companies as two halves that will come together to create an even better, more beautiful whole. Commonalities are played up, and it seems like the future holds nothing but sunshine and rainbows.

If only this were true. Unfortunately, some synergies never materialize. I spoke with a leader whose merger brought together three different printing companies. The people orchestrating the merger thought the three could live in perfect printing harmony, sharing equipment and materials to lower costs and increase revenue. But the companies had totally different priorities and timelines for serving customers. The company serving high-end customers felt they were creating art, so timelines weren't their focus. The company that made brochures needed decisions made quickly or they would miss their print and ship deadline. It became clear that since their clients were different, they used their equipment differently. Though they benefited from certain printing synergies, such as optimizing the use of the equipment during downtime, the difference in how they served their customers diminished the synergies they initially expected.

Synergies can also fail to materialize when merging companies offer complimentary products, but customers of one business don't or won't convert to the other. As an example, one interviewee worked for a company that provided employee surveys, about half of which were in healthcare. A PE firm acquired this company and merged it with a patient survey company, thinking there were opportunities to share resources and equipment while allowing clients to use one company for both employee and patient surveys. It quickly became clear that the employee survey business is very different from the patient survey business due to government regulations, client priorities, and more. The newly formed company declined for several years and was then sold to another firm.

Lack of expected synergies can be aggravating. Here again you can be a hero (and the post-M&A deal environment needs heroes). Perhaps the expected synergies don't materialize, but you might see other areas where working together can gain efficiencies. Leverage your expertise and knowledge to find new, unexpected synergies. As a frontline leader or team member, you have the best view on the day-to-day operations. Perhaps you've thought of or even suggested new procedures in the past. Now is the time to explore that idea with your new colleagues and see what works best.

## Be prepared

These threats to M&A success are pervasive. It can be next to impossible to avoid them. That said, anticipating these inevitable challenges (and others) can make all the difference. But you need to prepare. Whether you're going through M&A now or suspect you'll go through it soon, preparation will impact not only your morale, but your ability to navigate change and thrive.

Remember, by their nature, most organizations are somewhat dysfunctional. No matter what happens or how things seem to go downhill, no company starts off perfect. M&A isn't an art or science; there isn't one exact formula for all situations. Things need to be tweaked as you go along, and to do that, you need to pay attention and remain flexible. Try to understand how big-picture issues trickle down and permeate different layers of an organization. Make an effort to see others' perspectives. Open your eyes to opportunities to make things better for yourself, your coworkers, and your company. Ultimately, by recognizing issues down the line and reacting quickly, you can carve out your perfect niche at the newly merged company.

# SECTION 2

The M&A Stages
of Grief

# Introduction

**P**erhaps rumors have been flying for months, even years. Maybe the news came out of nowhere. Or maybe there's been no news at all, but you suspect your company is an M&A target. Whatever the case, you are wondering what all this means. Specifically, what it means to you.

This nagging unknown can settle in regardless of the state of your company. That unsettling feeling can start at the first whiff that a deal may be in the works. You sense something big is happening, but you just aren't sure if it's good or bad. And it's hard to tell when you will know.

You ask yourself, "What does this mean for me and my job?" (Possibly with an expletive thrown in there.) Together, we can find the answer. But first, I've got to be honest, it's going to be an emotional journey. This section will help you understand this journey, and hopefully make the path a little easier, no matter where you find yourself.

After a deal is announced, many M&A survivors describe their emotions as if they had gone through a breakup. The news feels like the death of a relationship, and really, it was. And like most relationships, we often don't realize how important the relationship we have with our company is until it is gone.

Elisabeth Kübler-Ross, M.D, famously coined the term "The Stages of Grief" in her groundbreaking book *On Death and Dying* (1969). In it she outlines the phases of grief experienced by those who learn they are dying.[14] She brilliantly identified how people feel, think, and act when faced with extreme loss. The truth is, after a deal is announced and things start to change, it can feel like you've lost a loved one.

When I was going through M&A, once I understood that my sadness was from grieving the "loss" of my company, and that there would be stages, I was relieved because it helped me see a way forward. I stopped questioning my sanity and started focusing on how to get through the stages.

What are the stages? Well, it starts with denial. Then there's anger, bargaining, depression, and acceptance. I've seen different terms applied for the stages in the middle, but most would agree—you start at denial and need to get to acceptance.

I can't assume to know how you feel, nor do I want to project on you what I went through. You might not experience all of these stages, or in this order, but I'm confident you'll experience some of them. Transitions are emotional, and I want you to know you're not going crazy. Let me shed a little light on the stages and how each helps you move forward:

- **Denial:** In denial, you refuse to believe this whole M&A thing is happening. You are convinced that things will fall apart and that this is a temporary distraction. The unspoken reality? Even if the merger or acquisition does not go through, things can never go back to the way they were. Appreciate that reality and move forward.

- **Anger**: Identify the anger you may experience once you realize the future you had envisioned has been altered. Understand that while feelings of anger are understandable and a sign that you have moved past denial, it's important to move past your anger in order to see opportunity.

- **Bargaining**: In this stage you may experience the flip-flop effect—flipping back and forth between embracing the new way of doing things and bargaining to keep things the way they were. It's a constant struggle. Understand why it happens and lean into the new way of doing things.

- **Depression**: At this stage you've realized there's no going back. You are slowly accepting the change, recognizing there is no stopping it. It is critical to appreciate the need to grieve completely, but to also let go so you can take steps toward acceptance.

- **Acceptance**: Getting to acceptance is key. Acceptance is defined for what it is: forgiveness of everyone and everything that changed, forgiveness so that you can embrace change, accept the situation, and decide whether to make it work or move on.

The following chapters will cover each stage in greater detail. I recommend reading the following (short) chapters in order to help you understand the full picture of M&A grief. If you feel emotionally stuck in a certain section, go on to the next. Seeing where you're going can help you better comprehend where you are, and you can always reread chapters as you work toward emotional progress.

It was a watershed moment once I understood that I ultimately needed to reach acceptance. This doesn't mean you have to agree with everything that's happened, but you have to *accept* that it has. Once you come to terms with a situation beyond your control, you're in a better position to see clearly and seize the opportunities ahead of you. The next section will help you get through each of these stages. You are not alone on this journey. I've got your back.

# A Spotify™ playlist for your grief stages

As your partner and guide through your work relationship breakup, I went ahead and created a 30-tune playlist on Spotify called *From Denial to Acceptance*. Yes, a playlist (and you're welcome). I don't know about you, but during my worst breakup there were certain songs or albums I played on repeat (mine all revolved around Anita Baker). When you go through a merger or acquisition, it can feel like you've been sucker punched, just like a bad breakup. Listening to certain songs can be cathartic, especially those that capture your mood and feeling. Hearing words that reflect how you feel reminds you that others have felt just as sad and mad as you.

As you read each of the stages and identify where you are, play the set of songs for that stage. It may help you get through that tough patch until you reach acceptance. While I'm pretty certain the songwriters did not write these songs with M&A deals in mind, they capture the sentiment. And remember, there's a whole mess of other songs written about new-found love and opening your heart to new possibilities. I'm just saying...

# Denial

The first stage of grief stinks. I spent enough time in denial during my first acquisition experience to know. While at first you may resist the emotional journey of M&A (the first stage *is* called denial), you need to take this journey to reach acceptance. But how do you begin?

Grief counselor Rita Bonchek says, "Grief is the act of mourning the future that won't be." Denial keeps you tethered to an imaginary future. It's hard accepting that the amazing future career you'd envisioned (aren't all future career dreams amazing?) might not play out the way you'd planned.

Don't despair. Your future has the potential to be better than you'd envisioned, *but that future won't happen if you hang out in denial*. Don't ignore how you feel. You likely had great dreams around your future career path, but hanging out in denial only hurts you.

What exactly are you mourning in this stage? Based on what I know and what others have shared with me, you may be mourning:

- the familiarity you enjoyed with your boss, your work colleagues, and your team

- the loss of a company culture that you loved and maybe even helped build

- the autonomy you had to make decisions and do your job

- the reality that people you worked with and admired may no longer be part of the future

- the certainty you felt when you woke up in the morning—for that day and the months (or years) ahead

Perhaps colleagues you enjoyed working with have moved into different roles or been let go. A dynamic company culture grows from daily moments spent with workmates. When that dynamic is ruptured, it can be enormously destabilizing. Breaking these threads and bonds is what makes the M&A experience so emotional.

This feeling of loss happens to companies on both sides, by the way. Remember that the acquiring company's employees are dealing with their own grief (whether you see it or not). The fact is they could not achieve their vision without you. They had to acquire to survive and grow.

Why is it important for you to get out of denial? Because there are opportunities you won't see if you're preoccupied with the things you've lost. Open up your mind to potential. It's the same advice I'd give to a friend in a breakup: "You've got to move on so you can meet someone with whom you can create an even better relationship." (I probably wouldn't say it that formally, but you get my point).

This new company is waiting to value you. Show them what you've got!

You may feel powerless to control your own destiny, like a pawn in someone else's game. You get caught up in managing the day to day—Who does what? Who takes lead? Who has final say? You just want to do your job, but you aren't even really sure what that is anymore. But keep one thing in mind:

**You are in charge of your destiny.**

While it'll take time to get over what you feel you've lost, you need to accept it and firmly decide how you want to move forward. Right now. Think about how you recovered after your toughest relationship breakup. Tissues, beer, and all. It took a while but over time you accepted it. You need to think about these stages as the end of one relationship—albeit a work one—and the start of a new one.

The first thing is to acknowledge what stage you're in. As the saying goes, "acknowledging the problem is half the solution." Do not deny you are in denial. It will help you realize that it is only a stage, a mere moment on your M&A journey.

The next step is to "mark the ending" [of your old ways].[15] I'm not encouraging you to burn his clothes in effigy on the front lawn or rip up her photos (okay, I may be taking this analogy too far), but it does help to acknowledge that, as successful as the old ways were, it is time to move on.

Marking the "ending" really helped my team and me. Before the acquisition, we would have a yearly gathering, with employees coming in from all over the globe, but the post-integration efforts had put it on hold. So instead we conducted a virtual global session with start times shifting daily to accommodate different time zones. We marked the ending by reviewing our old processes and systems to find which could contribute to the future while acknowledging that some no longer made sense. Doing it together bonded our team and allowed us to celebrate the work we'd done while exploring how our expertise would contribute to the future. The key was that we helped each other, together, step into what lay ahead and step out of denial.[16]

One interviewee who'd been through six M&A deals shared that, "Getting to acceptance is not so much about accepting what you now have but forgiving those who have changed your life. Getting past denial is letting go of bitterness."

Man, did I have a whole bucket o' bitter to let go of in my first acquisition experience. Fortunately, I realized that my pity party was only hurting me. You could say that my ex had moved on, yet I was stuck reliving my past successes over and over again. I finally realized I couldn't achieve any future success if I stayed stuck in a repeat loop of the old ones.

If you are struggling to get past denial, try to be honest with yourself; there were things about the old work relationship that could have been better. Perhaps there were archaic systems that could have been improved or standard operating procedures that no longer made sense. Now is your chance to re-evaluate where change and improvement can contribute to this new coupling and build a strong foundation for a new relationship with your company.

I hope this advice helps you move past denial and on to the next stage. But don't expect to move straight on to acceptance. There are plenty of other emotions you'll experience along the way. *And that's okay*. It's all part of the healing process. When I went through my M&As, I tended to accept the new company vision and get really excited about it. Yet when things started to go south, I would fall straight back into the arms of denial. Finally, I would move past it for good, and you will too. Take charge of your destiny.

*From Denial to Acceptance* Spotify™ Playlist, songs for the Denial Stage:

1. **Changes** - *David Bowie*
2. **Who are You?** - *The Who*
3. **(Don't Fear) the Reaper** - *Blue Oyster Cult*
4. **Send in the Clowns** - *Joan Collins*
5. **Would I Lie to You?** - *Annie Lennox/The Eurythmics*
6. **Manic Monday** - *The Bangles*

CHAPTER 5

# Anger

You probably have a lot to be angry about when it comes to M&A. Now, I'm not here to tell you that your emotions aren't real and valid. But being angry can keep you from realizing new opportunities and enjoying your job. Besides, anger doesn't really feel good, and it's not very productive either. This chapter is all about helping you get past the Anger Stage so you can get on with your career.

Let's first dissect the possible sources of your anger. An M&A deal—whether it has gone through or not—changes everything. If the deal is pending, then you likely foresee months of uncertainty, which is always frustrating. If the deal has gone through, now there are more people, systems, and processes to deal with just when you'd gotten to the point where you thought you knew the drill, and the short cuts and workarounds needed to get your stuff done. It's understandable to be angry about things that make your job harder or more complicated.

The times I've gone through M&A, I was always most angry when I thought about all of the personal sacrifices I'd made to help build up my company. Having to constantly answer questions from new people who second-guessed every previous decision was just plain aggravating. Then to see all that hard work unravel so quickly, undone by people who in my view had no clue what they were doing, just made my blood boil.

"Suddenly, people who were not around when you built the company are questioning decisions you made, forcing you to justify every action," shared one of my interviewees. "On top of that, they devalue the role of the people let go. So you are left doing their jobs knowing that no one understands how difficult or time consuming the work is. And don't even get me started when consultants are involved."

Perhaps some of the people you'd liked and admired have been forced out or let go. You witness rock stars (learn more about Former Rock Stars later) stumble because the metrics for success have changed. Any of this sound familiar? Your feelings are understandable, and venting will feel good—initially. If done for too long that rage can blind you to the opportunities before you. If all you focus on are the problems rather than on possible solutions, *you* will slowly become the problem.

Instead, keep pressing forward. This stage makes you no fun to be around, perhaps even detrimental, and you may get passed over for new opportunities because of it. If all people see when they look at you (besides the folded arms and snarky mutterings) is someone continuously railing against the deal, they won't think you are capable of contributing to the future, and that is *not* the image you want to paint. You will be evaluated on the value you bring to the new company, so if you remain perpetually angry, the perception of that value will be limited. As one interviewee told me, "Keep in mind, your leadership felt this M&A deal was both companies' best chance to succeed. You need to think about how you can contribute to that growth."

As with every stage, embrace your feelings, know that you are justified in having them, but don't dwell on them. You've got work to do. How to move on is the question. The key is letting go of the things you can't change and planning for those you can.

## From Anger to Action exercise

Write down all of the things that frustrate you. Think about your new situation and about the systems, processes, and general approaches that frustrated you before the M&A deal. Get it all out on paper. Next, you're going to sort these frustrations into two groups:

- Things that are out of your control
- Things you can potentially change, or at least influence, even if they aren't in your immediate control

If something is totally out of your control, don't waste emotional energy on it. Let it go. Don't carry the extra baggage. Take some deep breaths, do some meditation, picture the worries drifting away, and then cross them off your list.

With a bit of time and focus (perhaps in partnership with new team members), you can improve the situations you can control. It's going to take work, but it feels good to know there's a light at the end of the tunnel.

Do some brainstorming on these frustrations to start prioritizing your actions. How would changing these things better serve your customers? What about your colleagues? How could they contribute to the new vision? How could you take the lead to make improvements?

Finally, review this prioritized list with your boss or senior management and detail a path forward that addresses these issues. The best way to overcome anger is to channel it for good. Take action.

This exercise helped me get past the frustration of a slow creative review process. We were B2B, and the acquiring company was B2C. Our creative approach and output were very different. Our creative efforts stalled because they didn't understand our B2B approach. The delayed output was frustrating to us and our customers. Once we decided to involve the B2C team earlier in the creative process, it helped them understand our language and approach as we defined the objectives and strategy for the task ahead. This combined approach set the stage for this new creative approval process to become the standard for all our teams.

Chances are, if you're frustrated about something, you're not the only one. By identifying issues and creating plans for improvement, you become part of the solution. As a leader, this is part of your job. Leaders should serve as models for the behavior they want to see in their team. Letting go of anger is a key part of this.

One interviewee talked of his anger after being acquired,

having been in the role of acquirer in the past: "I realized though that the people below me were experiencing the same feelings of anger and that I needed to be the person to lead them out of it. Knowing I had to keep on a positive front, even though I had questions, actually helped me get through the stages. I had to do it for my team."

Get past your anger by focusing your energy on being a good leader. Know that anger is a common emotional reaction to M&A. It's easy to keep circling back to it on your journey to acceptance. Keep trying, and you will eventually get past it for good.

*From Denial to Acceptance* Spotify™ Playlist, songs for the Anger Stage:

1. Welcome to the Jungle - *Guns-N-Roses*
2. It's the End of the World as We Know It - *REM*
3. Take this Job and Shove it! - *Johnny Paycheck*
4. Money, Money, Money - *ABBA*
5. Who's Sorry Now? - *Connie Francis*
6. Set Fire to the Rain - *Adele*

# Bargaining

When I think about the bargaining I did during my fist acquisition, I have to laugh. Looking back, I wonder, "What was I thinking?" There was no way things were going back to how they were. But at the time, I thought I just had to make a credible case for how well something had worked in the past so that I could simply keep doing it that way while ostensibly embracing the change. Sound familiar?

You see, I was in the Bargaining Stage without realizing it. I hadn't yet had my epiphany. My first boss post deal (I had four within an 18-month period) equally liked things the way they had been. We were essentially codependents who enabled each other's bargaining efforts. I can look back on it now and think, "What a waste of time and energy!" But at the time, I felt like Joan of Arc on a crusade. I led the way with spectacular PowerPoints (my corporate weapon of choice), highlighting our past achievements and how we'd accomplished them. But all of those processes and procedures I held on to as "best practices" kept us mired in the past when we needed to be moving forward.

During the stages, you can feel like Don Quixote fighting

windmills. Each stage is exhausting—physically, mentally, and emotionally—in its own way. Bargaining can be even more exhausting because you're constantly going back and forth from trying to engage in new ways of doing things while looking for ways to preserve what you did. I call it the *flip-flop effect*. You are inching forward toward acceptance while devising ways to postpone the inevitable. It's understandable. If you've been acquired, you're thinking, "They acquired us because we've been successful at what we do, so why do we need to change?" And if you are the acquirer, you're thinking, "*We* acquired *you*. Clearly our way is better!"

According to one of my interviewees, endless bargaining almost killed several integrations of which he was a part. "In many integration scenarios I experienced ... each side competes to win. They bargain for their way to be what is chosen. So when you have people in the same room competing, trying to preserve their product rather than thinking about the long-term strategy or the customer, you get nowhere."

Both sides may waste time bargaining because they are each most comfortable with what they know and convinced it is the best way, especially when the individuals involved in the discussion were the authors of those same "best practices."

Keep in mind, *there was a reason your company entered into a merger or acquisition agreement with another company.* Your company leadership determined that survival meant you needed a partner. This means things cannot stay the way they were. That is the reality—for both sides.

The key to ending the bargaining spin cycle is to divorce yourself from how you have always done things in order to gain a clear understanding of what the new vision is, what you are now striving for, and how success will be measured within this new entity. Is it market share? Growth? Revenue? Be clear on these, and above all else, focus on what best serves your customer.

Don't waste that energy bargaining to hold on to the past. Instead, channel it toward creating a new way. I spent countless hours rationalizing why the old ways were best and looking for ways to prove it. This doesn't mean you "throw the baby out with the bath water." There may be many things you used to do that can contribute to the future, but you need to be flexible and look to adapt them to the new way. You need to be in learning mode, not bargaining mode. The more you learn about the new direction and train to have the right knowledge and skills to participate, the more you can contribute.

Also know that when the new strategy seems to be going off the rails, it doesn't mean things will revert back to how they once were (although you may pray for that to be the case). Not gonna happen. In fact, it's likely that things will just keep changing. One of my interviewees advised that leaders always be ready for the next wave. "There is the initial deal, and then months later a whole new restructure can happen because things are not working," she said. "Be prepared for that, but don't assume that means things will go back to the way they were. The company is now wed to its new strategy and is figuring out every way to make this new strategy stick. They won't be going back to the old."

As you accept this, and it may take a while, focus on co-creating new best practices with your colleagues that serve the company's vision and your customer. Find ways to work with the other side. At this stage, survival means being open-minded and flexible. Consider the past ideas you've had on how to improve processes or procedures and seize the opportunity to put them into action. Remember, you're building toward acceptance. Finding ways to fit in and adapt to the change may bring relief as you inch closer toward the inevitable.

*From Denial to Acceptance* Spotify™ Playlist, songs for the Bargaining Stage:

1. **Stuck in the Middle with You** - *Stealers Wheel*
2. **Give a Little Bit** - *Supertramp*
3. **Here We Go Again** - *Ray Charles & Nora Jones*
4. **Hard Day's Night** - *The Beatles*
5. **The Gambler ("know when to hold 'em, know when to fold 'em, know when to walk away ...)** - *Kenny Rogers*
6. **Should I Stay or Should I Go** - *The Clash*

YORK

# CHAPTER 7

# Depression

The best way to describe the initial feeling of this stage is "hollow." You have accepted that change is happening, but rather than feeling excitement and jubilation, you feel exhausted, like you just can't fight it anymore. This is the Depression Stage. It's a downer for sure. But with help from this book, my hope is you won't be here too long. And if you are reading this before reaching this stage and think you can avoid it—you can't.

You need to spend a little time in depression to truly move on to acceptance. If you rush through this stage or sidestep it, your step into acceptance will be half-hearted and you could very well slip back. But I'm going to help you get through it.

How did you get here? You've been frustrated and angry, and yet you've also had hope, bargaining to hold on to your old ways. But after flipping back and forth, trying to embrace the new while holding on to the old, you've slowly resigned yourself to the fact that there is no going back. The tough part is you are still unclear what exactly you are moving toward.

For some, this kind of shake-up can be exhilarating and exciting right from the get-go—and if you fall into this camp, God bless you. But if you are in the bigger camp of people who cast a wary eye on change and aren't so sure about all of this, then this stage is the most emotional. This stage comes cloaked in some of the yuckier feelings, like regret, guilt, and fear. A basic sadness sandwich.

It was in this Depression Stage that I found Kübler-Ross's stages of grief and William Bridge's *Surviving Corporate Transition*. It was a huge relief after reading these as I realized I was simply transitioning through depression. I thought I was going mad. I had inexplicable feelings of sadness, and people around me were acting so different, making me even sadder. The people I thought I knew started to seem like strangers. I felt like Donald Sutherland's character in the *Invasion of the Body Snatchers* remake slowly realizing my friends had been taken over by aliens.

"It's hard when you realize the company that acquired you does not value what you did or what you currently do," shared one of my interviewees who had been head of marketing. "Our acquiring company's view of marketing was that it was used for client entertainment. The new CEO did not get the strategy part of marketing or that marketing could actually contribute to revenue. He had built his company through serial acquisitions—*not* through marketing. I realized that he was entertaining my presentations to show sensitivity to the other company, but he had no interest in what marketing could do." This, by the way, was a refrain I heard during many of my interviews—that new leaders do not always value what you have been invested in—and that's hard to take.

With an undefined role as integration pressed onward, one interviewee was left asking, "What am I left with? When a number of people are let go and you are surrounded by empty offices, empty desks, rows of empty cubes ... it just heightens your depression."

How do you move past this stage? First, accept that you may be an emotional wreck for a bit and may even experience a good cry or two. But just like that big cry after a bad breakup, releasing your emotional energy can be followed by a sense of relief and a renewed energy for what's next. You need to let these feelings wash over you, and that includes letting them circle down the drain.

Another interviewee confessed, "The weekend after the news, I was an emotional wreck. I saw my dreams falling apart right in front of me. Or so I thought. It made me realize you need to always be ready for the possibility of anything to happen. That is the kind of mindset you need to have nowadays. M&A is now a natural part of business, and you need to always be prepared. "

This period in between, where you are letting go of the old yet not 100% into the new, is often called the "neutral zone." It was coined by William Bridges, who emphasized that transition can only start with an ending, a letting go of something. He believed that the gap between the old and the new is the time when innovation is most possible and when an organization can be revitalized.[17]

Defining what you seek moving forward helps you stop thinking about what you lost and focuses your energy on what you want next. What helped me get out of my neutral zone was to form a picture in my mind of the future I wanted. To continue the breakup analogy, you must start to define your next ideal partner. Doing this exercise will help you see that you can love again. And then write it down to make it a reality.

- What are you looking for in a future (work) relationship?
- What would make you fulfilled?
- What would bring out the best in you?
- What are things you didn't like that you can improve on?
- What are things you have wanted to learn at work but haven't had the time or opportunity to pursue?

Be creative. Think big. Writing down your answers crystallizes what you want and provides purpose and direction. You'll start to see the possibilities for a new beginning.

Above all, take it easy at this stage. Don't make rash decisions. Your thoughts may be a bit blurry as you waver between embracing new ways of thinking while not wanting to lose the type of thinking that made you, you. It's not good to make potentially life-altering decisions when you're depressed. Resist. Get to acceptance first. Then, with a clearer, less emotional perspective, you can start making smarter decisions.

***From Denial to Acceptance*** Spotify™ Playlist,
songs for the Depression Stage:

1. **Who Am I?** - *Les Misérables* (Hugh Jackman,
   Motion Picture version - because who doesn't like
   Hugh?)
2. **Over my Head** - *Fleetwood Mac* (or *Echosmith*
   version)
3. **Catch my Breath** - *Kelly Clarkson*
4. **These Days** - *Rudimental*
5. **Lonely Together** - *Avicii*
6. **All by Myself** - *Eric Carmen*

YORK

CHAPTER 8

# Acceptance

With acceptance as the final stage on your M&A journey through grief, you may be expecting to end this roller-coaster ride in wild celebration, maybe even dancing jubilantly in your office with a glass of champagne to toast your emotional progress. It's a beautiful vision, and you should absolutely celebrate how far you've come, but based on my experience and research, arriving at acceptance rarely results in dancing. Though you have made it here, which truly should be considered a personal victory, it likely still feels a bit hollow.

As Kübler-Ross wrote, "Acceptance should not be mistaken for a happy stage—it is almost void of feelings."[18] It seems odd, given how emotional some of the previous stages are, like anger and depression, but trust me, being devoid of feeling is not unusual. Getting to acceptance does not mean you have to agree with what's happened; you simply have to accept that it has. It can feel almost anticlimactic. You may even ask yourself, "why all the fuss? What was I fighting against so badly?" You stop denying the change or bargaining for ways to keep things as they were.

One of my interviewees said, "One day I finally realized that what I had been fighting for seemed such a colossal waste of energy. As the head of marketing, I was continually getting triggered by the other company's lack of respect for our nomenclature, our branding, our culture. But after a while, I couldn't figure out what had been making me so frustrated. I had slowly come to acceptance and had stopped internalizing all of the changes as a personal affront to what my team and I had built."

The good news is that once you get to acceptance you tend not to revert back to any of the other stages. You have finally accepted that the change is permanent (as permanent as change can be these days). Now you need to focus. *You need to get on with getting on.* Make sense of your new organization's expectations to help you fully commit to the change and achieve success. As I shared in the last chapter, you are now officially in the neutral zone. You have let go of the old way while smack in the middle of trying to figure out what your new way looks like. You've become tired of the ambiguity.

At this stage you don't want to make any hasty decisions. All this change that seems to have thrown everything you knew into a tailspin might have you wanting to jump ship, but be patient. Starting over somewhere else will still require a whole new level of investment. Ideally, you have built up some equity at your company. You know how to get things done, who to go to for certain things, and you've built up a positive reputation with your colleagues. Remember, you have time invested with your company. The grass may look greener on the other side, but sometimes when you go to that grassier side, it turns out to be AstroTurf.

Patience is important, but it needs to be balanced with an earnest effort on your part to figure out what's next. As I have said before, the key is to always know your value. Once you are clear on your value and your desires, consider all the ways that value can contribute to the new future. If you do determine that where your company is going no longer aligns with your values and interests, then begin deliberately crafting a new future path.

This was the reality that one of my interviewees faced. She was the CMO at a start-up that merged with another company. Their cultures were wildly different, and she saw the other company's culture starting to overtake hers. She recalled, "I left because I had accepted what had happened, but I was not happy with it and I knew it wasn't going to change. It was never going back to the way it had been. The new vision no longer aligned with my desires, and I determined it was time for me to go. But I made this decision over time because I wanted to feel I had truly given it my all."

The new beginning will only take place after people have come through the wilderness and are ready to make the emotional commitment to do things the new way. If I go back to Kübler-Ross' observations, acceptance doesn't mean you will forget the person you lost or that moving on with your life dishonors them. It is simply an acknowledgement that how things were will no longer be and it's time to create that new life. The same applies in a business setting. It is time to shape your career path in a way that capitalizes on your value and allows you to continue to grow and learn.

One of my interviewees had headed a business development team when his company was acquired by a smaller competitor. "After getting past the agony, frustration, and uncertainty, I started to realize that the new company had a different business approach that actually put my team in a more enviable position," he said. "In my prior company's business model, we were the low-margin business, but in the new company we were seen as having high-margin potential. We went from the black sheep to the white sheep. Once you get past your anger and get to acceptance, it allows your brain to see that good things can happen."

As I shared at the very beginning, sometimes the stages of M&A grief do not progress in a linear fashion. It gets messy. But emotions are messy, and life is messy. And post-deal integration? It's the definition of messy. But working through these stages sets you up for success. It helps you frame what you really want in the next go around. Stay positive and focused and have the right attitude and you will get through it. Remember, millions of us have been through what you are going through. Know your value and you'll be okay. Promise.

*From Denial to Acceptance* Spotify™ Playlist, songs for the Acceptance Stage:

1. **Always Look on the Bright Side of Life** - *Monty Python's "The Life of Brian"*
2. **When the Going Gets Tough, the Tough Get Going** - *Billy Ocean*
3. **You Can't Always Get What You Want** - *The Rolling Stones*
4. **Ray of Light** - *Madonna*
5. **Let it Be** - *The Beatles*
6. **That's Life!** - *Frank Sinatra*

# SECTION 3

The Post-M&A Deal
Cast of Characters

# Introduction

In the previous section, I talked about the M&A stages of grief and shared how to figure out what stage you are in by identifying the feelings and emotions you are experiencing. Now I want to bring to life the personalities that emerge when you go through a merger or an acquisition. This is less about *how you are feeling* and more about *what you are seeing* in the people around you.

Every M&A deal results in a new set of bosses and work colleagues, but even former co-workers can be a source of unruly and unforeseen personality shifts. People change to accommodate the new regime, and the change in behavior can be destabilizing. Always keep in mind that everyone (which means people from both sides) is wondering what their future role will be. This can create a "survival of the fittest" environment, even within your once-familiar office. I'll prepare you for how your colleagues may change and how former allies may become different animals once their survival instincts get the best of them.

In true "field guide" fashion, all of the 10 characters have an illustration. I want you to be able to identify each one on sight, because you may feel like you're out in the wild sometimes. So, when you see illustrations like the Ostrich, I am pretty confident you're going to think, "Oh, I know who this is." On that note, I want you to keep two things in mind: First, although the illustrations are gender specific, each character could be any gender. Second, while the illustrations are caricatures, and might make you laugh (ideally), I do not judge these personalities negatively or positively, nor should you. The truth is, you are likely going to recognize that *you* have acted in some of the ways I describe. When people are in survival mode, they are prone to doing things they would never normally do, since primal "fight or flight" instinct takes over.

My goal here is to help you identify the personality types and know what to expect so you can be a better manager of your work product, your team, and your career decisions. I want you to be able to figure out if one of your colleagues has become a Black Widow. I want you to be able to keep your cool and find a way to collaborate with a Know-It-All (a character you encounter frequently in an M&A situation) before you throttle his neck.

Similar to being in the wilderness, not all animals—I mean characters—are equal in terms of the threat they pose. The characters I have identified fall on a spectrum. Some of your colleagues might just have a few predispositions of a character type, whereas others might take it to an extreme. Usually, people start out with minor tendencies that can spiral into something bigger—especially in an environment where fear is the operating agenda. This is problematic because it creates a highly dysfunctional workplace.

This section will help you recognize the kinds of crazy behaviors and actions that can make the "people part" of

M&A deals rough, so you know what to expect and how to find your path. And if you see yourself in a character, you'll understand how to manage your tendencies and evolve into the best person you can be.

# CHAPTER 9

# The Former Rock Star

During any business transformation, a person's perceived value at a company can fluctuate. These fluctuations are especially dramatic during a merger or acquisition because the people in charge tend to change, and the goals, mission, and direction of the company can evolve as well.

In post-deal situations, you might have a leader who was well-loved by a CEO, but if that CEO is no longer in charge, that leader's perceived value can dim quickly. Or you could have a product development whiz who was valued for driving your product line, but if there's a strategy shift after the acquisition, that leader may no longer be pulled into certain product meetings. This is how someone goes from being a Rock Star to a Former Rock Star.

Rock Stars can come from anywhere in the company. They can be high up the ladder or high-potential leaders on track to advance. They can be sales leaders, marketing gurus, or industry specialists. They can be the innovators everyone goes to for new ideas or the high performers winning all of the awards at sales banquets.

So how does a Rock Star become a Former Rock Star?

When big strategy change happens, as is typical post-M&A deal, the landscape shifts. Suddenly, what Rock Stars thought was important and valued at the company seems to have changed, and they struggle with redefining their role in this new world. This produces some complicated emotions for people not ready for the change. In other words, they keep insisting on playing hard rock when everyone else has moved on to disco. For Rock Stars who have a hard time pivoting, these emotions can be crippling.

If their emotions get the better of them, Rock Stars can stay stuck in denial. Their way of doing things worked well before; it's what made them successful. They are reluctant to change because their formula is what got them to where they are. Why change? Who is to say any other way is better? They believe this new way surely won't succeed. It's just so counter to how they have done things. They want to be ready for when everyone finally agrees and goes back to the old way of doing things, and then they can say, "I told you so."

The tough part is that their perceived value at the company was based on the prior success metrics—the old way of doing things. Now with strategies shifting, new success metrics are being defined. Now those once super-confident Rock Stars are having a difficult time adjusting to the new metrics for success. The key will be in their ability to pivot and adapt their contributions for the new company and its new direction.

A Former Rock Star is usually pretty easy to identify, but just in case, here are variations of phrases they might say to help you spot them:

- "I've been the top salesperson for the last three years (or I launched our last three product successes, etc.) Why would I change how I do things? You all can do what you want, but I'm sticking to what I know works."

- "I've been an integral part of what made this company successful. You mean to tell me that my approach, which made us a valuable company, is no longer valued?"

- "It's just a matter of time before I am proven right and we go back to the old way of doing things. You'll see."

Here are some actions you may witness that will help you identify Former Rock Stars:

- Complains openly that the changes (whatever they are) are wrong and a waste of time.

- Sulks in a corner, arms folded, stewing in meetings or won't show up at all for meetings that focus on the new way of doing things.

- Becomes reclusive as he sees that he is no longer revered.

I interviewed a finance leader at a company who was used to being the acquirer. His team was admired in the company because the CEO counted on finance to drive their acquisition strategy. Then their company was acquired by a smaller competitor. The finance leader was blindsided. In his mind it should have been the other way around. His behavior was that of a Former Rock Star. He confessed he was stuck in denial for a while, and he had a hard time shifting his mindset. He even called the former CEO of his company to vent about how things were changing.

Eventually, he realized he could either get on board with the new way of doing things or find another job. He recognized the new opportunities in front of him and became more accepting of change. For example, there were growth areas his team had identified in the past, but they never had the time or resources to explore them. Under this new company, new leaders might have different interests and priorities. Through this shift in mindset he was able to pivot and become a key contributor to the new vision.

### What if *you* are the Former Rock Star?

How do I break this to you? You need to pivot. I know you're thinking that things will eventually go back to the way they were, but they won't. This M&A deal happened for a reason. I may not know the drivers for your deal, but I know it was done because it was considered the best viable option for growth. Think about what you were able to achieve before and consider how you can contribute your expertise to this new company. It can be tough to let go of your old approach and identity, but your survival and happiness depend on it.

The Rock Star who pivots successfully recognizes that the new vision means a new way of doing things or adapting an expertise to contribute in new ways. M&A requires everyone to be open to change. It's hard, but it's the way to make M&A actually work. When people resist getting on board, they're going to be miserable as everyone pivots around them, and they usually won't last long. If you can help nudge someone toward the new way of doing things, you are doing a favor to that person and the company overall.

As clichéd as it sounds, keep one thing in mind: "You can lead a horse to water, but you can't make him drink." Whether Former Rock Stars are your colleagues or boss, they have to change their mindset on their own—you can't force it. In fact, you don't want them taking you down with them. Former Rock Stars tend to look for allies who support them and how they have always done their work. Unfortunately, allying with them can damage your image post M&A, especially if they have been vocal about their displeasure. You need to distance yourself from those who can't get on board with the new direction.

So what can you do in the short term when working with Former Rock Stars? Remember, the success of Former Rock Stars will come from pivoting, so you don't want to do or say things that keep them stuck in the past:

- **Don't flatter or indulge their old way of doing things**. It just feeds the beast.
- **Don't avoid or ignore them.** Show them through your behavior that it's time to move on.
- **Don't kick them when they are down.** Now is not the time to gloat over their misery. Your most important character trait post acquisition is your integrity.

Beyond just what you say, showing Former Rock Stars what success looks like can nudge them in the right direction. Here are three steps I recommend if they're colleagues you like (if you don't, I assume this requires no explanation).

1.   Acknowledge that how they used to do things before was amazingly successful, but the new vision requires new approaches and new thinking.
2.   Point out ways the approach or method they previously pursued could be adapted and evolved.
3.   Show them how you are modifying your old way of doing things to benefit the new vision. Lead by example.

If the mindset shift and pivot isn't happening by step three, you need to move on. They aren't likely to survive much longer.

When Former Rock Stars are higher up the career ladder than you, this one's a bit more delicate. It really depends on the type of relationship you have. If it's a good one and you think they just need a nudge to pivot, I recommend the above three steps. After that, it's up to them; there's nothing else you can do. If it's not a good relationship, and they were a "pain in the arse" as a Rock Star then you probably really don't care, right? "What goes around comes around," as they say.

In a strange way, M&A gives people a fresh start and levels the playing field. Everyone has another chance at a first impression with new leaders and colleagues, and it shakes up the status quo. In general, this is positive. But when people were considered Rock Stars at the original company, they might be feeling insecure if they aren't getting the same level of respect and attention. Sometimes these feelings become public, and sometimes people keep it bottled up. Have compassion as people adapt to changing roles and priorities. This is a hard time for everyone.

CHAPTER 10

# The Great Unifier

Every organization has a favorite senior leader or two. They are the leaders who almost everyone likes. They are smart, compassionate bosses who bring value to the company individually while also inspiring teams to do their best. People enjoy working for them. Comments like "they are my favorite boss" are not uncommon. Great galvanizers of teams roll up their sleeves to contribute to the work and consistently bring people together to take pride in what's been achieved. When a merger or acquisition occurs, they are the leaders people are drawn to for advice. They are stable and level-headed and have empathy for the emotions people are experiencing. Every acquisition has to have at least one hero, and this is usually found (or at least wished for) in the Great Unifier.

When a merger or acquisition occurs, Great Unifiers command a lot of respect. People want to hear what they think. ("Is this merger a good thing? What does it mean for the company?") Since Great Unifiers are about bringing people together to do their best work, they are the leaders most actively showing enthusiasm for the deal, trying to get everyone on board, and highlighting the enormous potential for the new company and what it all means for the future.

People really want to get on board with Great Unifiers and trust in what they're saying. They have been such great leaders in the past, people want to keep trusting and following them. But unfortunately, it's not that simple. And here's where this character gets caught in the drama.

With mergers and acquisitions, the power balance shifts. While Great Unifiers were respected leaders in the original company, when companies come together it's a whole new ballgame. A ballgame where the rules constantly change as a company shifts from the old way of doing things to a new, yet-to-be-defined way. As cultures compete, the work atmosphere can go from peaceful jungle to survival of the fittest. And to survive you need to be ready to play a game where the rules are defined as you go along. If Great Unifiers, who have been valued and respected for their compassionate leadership, don't pick up on these shifts, it can be their undoing.

People so desperately want to share in the enthusiasm and optimism of Great Unifiers, but they also don't want to be duped. Given the poor success rate of M&A deals, the imprint on most people's collective brains is negative. They don't trust anyone or anything because they've heard the horror stories. They would like to continue following Great Unifiers, but now they are watching a cast of other characters circling around. Post deal, as people assess what's true and what isn't, they are trying to determine if Great Unifiers' leadership is still effective or if they've unwittingly become naïve chumps. People are trying to decide which horse to back and they aren't sure whether Great Unifiers will survive this game.

"Beware of naïve optimism," revealed an interviewee who experienced a multibillion-dollar media acquisition. "From my experience, mergers and acquisitions are a ruthless business. My best advice? You have to be a healthy pessimist instead of a constant optimist—and I say this as someone who's always been an optimist. You need to be savvy. You can't be a pawn."

The crux of the issue is that Great Unifiers are not focused on being politically savvy. They haven't had to be. They've been good at their job, and their leadership brand has been about believing and trusting in people. They understood the rules of the game because they actively contributed to creating that positive culture. But here's the problem: in the post-deal landscape, the rules automatically change as different cultures come together. People are trying to determine which culture will prevail—and compassionate leadership usually doesn't end up on top. At least not at the beginning.

Whether you are the Great Unifier or are working for one, how can you maintain your integrity, and your compassionate leadership, without being consumed by the politics? How do you quickly get smart on the politics being played so you understand the new rules and who or what is driving them? From my experience, there are two things you need to do:

1. Listen very carefully to company communications.
2. Actively "read between the lines" on responses.[19]

Some might suggest a third, which is to dig around amongst peers for more intelligence, but this is risky because it can be hard to discern fact from gossip and conjecture in the early days. Best to draw your own conclusions from what you hear and see.

Listening to *what* leadership communicates and *how* they communicate provides an enormous amount of invaluable insight. *What* a leader says can have several layers of meaning, and *how* it is said can be a giveaway to various subtexts. In a post-M&A deal environment, you are looking for subtext. For instance, if executives give you a routine, generic answer without showing any passion, then you can typically conclude they are just towing the corporate line. The flipside is true as well. If they answer enthusiastically off-the-cuff, then you can conclude they are really behind the effort. These observations are equally invaluable.

Beyond just listening, actively reading between the lines means that not only do you understand what is being said, you also pick up on what is being articulated outside of words. Pay attention to people's body posture, voice tone, gestures, and how they subtly react to questions asked by you or others. In an M&A environment where you might witness a lot of disingenuous behavior, taking the time to read between the lines can be a valuable skill. You will be amazed at how much more you can learn.

"We could tell that enthusiasm for our product launch had diminished just by the way our leadership talked about it," revealed one of my interviewees who'd experienced several multibillion-dollar acquisitions and considered himself a Great Unifier. "While they said it was still a key part of the portfolio moving forward, we saw in how they essentially avoided discussing it until asked that it had dropped in importance. It was a key lesson for me as the leader of my team to not take anything at face value anymore."

It's not that you can't trust anything you hear; you just have to be smart about the questions you ask. Smart listening requires smart questions. Take the time to formulate strong questions to provide the most valuable insights and follow these guidelines to be an active listener skilled at reading between the lines.[20]

1. **Take in what has been said, but also pay attention to what has not been said.** For example, in a discussion about a product launch you might note that something was not covered. To dig, you can ask something like, "I noticed that in our discussion, you didn't mention XYZ. Should I interpret that to mean this is no longer important?"

2. **Recognize when people are deliberately avoiding an issue that they should typically be addressing.** If an executive is routinely avoiding discussing a certain project or topic that she would typically discuss, that's a sign that something is up and it's worth getting smarter on.

3. **Pay close attention not just to what people say but the way in which they say it.** If they answer enthusiastically or in a monotone fashion, both responses provide significant insight.

The value of taking the time to read between the lines helps you understand what leadership really wants. The key is you are always looking for subtext—the message behind the message.

## How to handle "land-grabbers" if you are the Great Unifier

In my three acquisition experiences, I have consistently played the role of Great Unifier. It is a great and critical role to play, but you have to stay smart and appreciate the power shifts happening. If you don't, you can get duped, and your team won't follow you. They have no choice. They will see other leaders or teams who seize on the post-deal chaos to gain more responsibilities, who "land-grab" even if it is not their area of expertise. They may grab for responsibilities that are legitimately yours. You should expect this and plan for it. Follow the above advice—listen carefully, read between the lines, and proactively demonstrate your expertise at every opportunity.

A deal's success relies on people staying engaged and productive, and no one is better at getting that from teams than the Great Unifier. But they have to be tapped in and stay smart on what is really going on in the company. This includes effectively listening to their team. By nature of being on the front lines, team members can often see some of the shifts happening better than the Great Unifier can. To truly be effective, the Great Unifier must create meaningful, ad hoc opportunities with teams and individuals to get a sense of what they are thinking, seeing, and experiencing. The more the Great Unifier knows—not just from senior leadership but from how their team(s) are embracing the post-deal changes—the better leader a Great Unifier can be to make change truly happen.

CHAPTER 11

# The Know-It-All

We *all* know Know-It-Alls. You don't need a merger or an acquisition to meet or work with one. These are the "been there, done that" type of people. They've never met a question, problem, or challenge for which they didn't think they had the answer, even if they have no qualified expertise on the subject matter. They monopolize the conversation (why bother to listen to anyone else?) and make business decisions without all of the necessary input because they typically haven't bothered to ask. And according to professional psychologists, they honestly do believe they know everything.[21]

You can spot them in meetings fairly quickly. They tend to be vocal early on, pointing out everything they have done or led and how it was successful (because they never highlight their failures). They ooze an "I really don't feel like I can learn anything from you" energy.

The tough part is when this personality is part of the post-deal integration because their tendency to act like they know everything can cripple any efforts at collaboration. They are more focused on showing you how much they know rather than learning from you. They don't even fake interest in wanting to get your thoughts or ideas. And that does not bode well for deal success, which relies on teams coming together and sharing knowledge to make things work.

"During the post-deal integration, we had a new boss come over to lead our marketing team," shared one of my interviewees. "He had been head of marketing and sales at the prior company, and we picked up right away that he thought he knew everything. But honestly, he didn't know anything about marketing. He'd really been sales focused without developing a marketing strategy. He chose not to capitalize on the expertise of our marketing team, and I suspect he was worried he'd be uncovered as a fraud. What made it worse was that he was a micro-manager. He didn't have enough confidence not to be involved in everything."

When the Know-It-All comes over from the other side you may wonder to yourself during discussions, "Why the hell did you acquire our company since you seem to know everything?" The truth is their company doesn't know it all—and deep down, they know it. (Even if a few individuals are delusional on this fact.) I go back to my consistent theme: this M&A deal happened for a reason. Your two companies needed each other to grow.

I'm no psychotherapist, but my general assessment (contributed to by my interviews) is that Know-It-Alls tend to be highly insecure and they compensate by acting like they know everything. Further insight reveals that they are afraid of not being good enough. They don't ever want to look like they are out of the loop, uneducated, or un-informed. The tough part is that in M&A deals there are bound to be periods of time where people are out of the loop because the loop is still being figured out.

In their desire to look smart and be appreciated for all that they can do, Know-It-Alls actually begin to aggravate people because it becomes apparent over time that they are not the experts they present themselves to be. They then begin to shut out people who actually do know what they are doing in a given area.

"A lot of people position themselves as important at the beginning of an integration because they don't want to lose their job," revealed an interviewee who worked in the restaurant business. "But they act like they know everything in areas where they truly do not have the expertise. Rather than acknowledge those who do have the experience, they act like they have it."

In her case, having too many people acting like Know-It-Alls killed a deal's potential for success. "Too many people left or lost their jobs because new leaders didn't know or take the time to understand what they did. Yet the Know-It-Alls who stayed had little value to contribute. They used big words to appear smart but truly knew nothing. It killed the deal success because it took a while to see through these people."

The Know-It-All doesn't need to come over from the other company. Many times, I witnessed fellow work colleagues who acted as though they knew how to do many other people's roles to keep a job or to create a new job for themselves.

"We had a Global Sales Kick-Off, and the people put in charge were people I'd worked with," shared one of my interviewees. "They presented themselves as knowing how to do it all when I knew they didn't. They allowed no other point of view because they wanted to look like they had everything under control to the new company leadership. So, they shut out former work colleagues who actually had more experience. It was hard because we'd previously partnered well together. It was no longer about making the team look good; it became all about making themselves look good."

If somehow you aren't sure you are dealing with a Know-It-All (though highly unlikely you can't tell), here are a few phrases that can help you identify one:

- "Oh, we explored that already. It was a complete waste of our time. We don't need to bother considering that option."

- "The reason that won't work is because of the velocity of change and the magnitude of effort coupled with the precision timing required to make it work is not achievable (You say—huh?!? This is an example of using big words that mean nothing to sound smart.)

- "You don't know what you are talking about. The way you do it is blah, blah, blah..."

Now, you could just throw up your hands and say, "I give up! Not worth my time to deal with this blow-hard!" when dealing with a Know-It-All. But you don't want their character traits to undermine your potential for success. There are ways to deal with Know-It-Alls that can enable you to be successful and maybe, even possibly, begin to collaborate with them in a productive way. Let's explore how to deal with a Know-It-All and what to do differently if the Know-It-All is your new boss versus a new work colleague.

## What if YOU are the Know-It-All?

Are you noticing that you tend to be the one talking most in meetings? Do you find yourself formulating your answer while others are talking? Are you spending more time looking to show off your knowledge and less time acknowledging others' expertise? Chances are you are acting like a Know-It-All. I'm not going to psychoanalyze why. There could be a variety of reasons. But I can tell you it is hurting your chances to be successful. You might think that success in the post-deal world is showing how smart you are. That's only half of it. M&A success is a team sport. If others don't feel heard, they'll stop contributing or worse, stop inviting you to discussions. You can't afford either. Think about your end goal. Post deal, showing how well you work with others sets you up better for success than always showing you are the smartest person in the room.

If the Know-It-All is your new boss, it can be delicate. You are trying to share what you know and how you can contribute to the new company vision when you may feel like all you ever hear back is "I've already done that" or "I don't think that's necessary." Here are tips on how to handle Know-It-All bosses:[22]

1. **Be smart on facts**. The more armed you are with unique knowledge and facts, and sources to back it up, the harder it is for your boss to interject and challenge your expertise. The better prepared you are, the harder it is for them to take over. And you may eventually earn their respect, because for them, knowledge is power.

2. **Don't fight every battle**. Battling with Know-It-Alls can be exhausting because you will never convince them they are wrong. And if it's your new boss, do you really want to risk your role proving she doesn't know what she is talking about? Odds are you don't win that battle even if you are right. Save your energy and choose a moment where you truly are the expert and can engage her productively with your knowledge. See above to do this right.

3. **Make 'em laugh!** When you think about it, Know-It-Alls are likely not just aggravating you, but others as well. Their need to be smarter applies to everyone. So if you don't take it as a personal affront, using laughter can diffuse almost any situation. But avoid the temptation for the sarcastic laugh. You want to laugh with them, not at them.

Now if the Know-It-All is your new work colleague or subordinate, the above still applies, but there are a few more tactics you can employ:

1. **Lead by example**. Know-It-Alls believe they need to demonstrate they know everything. Show that it's okay not to know everything. Saying, "I don't know but let's figure it out together," can help build trust and show you don't expect them to know everything.

2. **Ask questions.** To temper the behavior of Know-It-Alls, teach them that they need to come prepared. Ask probing questions and ask for their source. This need not be done in a snarky way (you are trying to foster collaboration), but in a genuine, professional way. Do this enough and they will either come prepared or will stop interjecting.

3. **Employ laughter**. See above; the same good advice applies.

Having the humility to listen and ask for help, and providing help when asked, is a critical piece in a deal's success. Too many deals are undone and fail because of arrogance. And often that arrogance is reflected by a Know-It-All. The key to success in every deal is having humility, acknowledging that you need each other and can learn from each other. As we've covered, an M&A deal's success requires that each side come to the deal with respect for the other. It's that simple.

# CHAPTER 12

# The Know-Nothing

The flip side to the Know-it-All is the Know-Nothing. Discerning this personality type is a little trickier than might first be assumed. You could think, "Well, if they know nothing, isn't that fairly obvious?" Yes and no.

Know-Nothings are often nice people who are agreeable and easy to get along with. And in the sea of problematic post-M&A personalities, these aren't the people making the biggest waves. That's why it's easy to overlook them in the beginning. But after multiple meetings, conference calls, and one-on-one discussions, you begin to wonder how these people provide any value to the company. You might also wonder how they were hired in the first place. Perhaps they were helpful and productive at one point, but they haven't evolved with the role. It's also possible that they were never really all that helpful, but they haven't done anything that warrants termination. Know-Nothings can be found at all levels of the company, and they often stick around for the long haul.

In any situation where you have to collaborate with others, working with Know-Nothings is tough. You are likely to feel like these people aren't pulling their own weight. But it's a tricky situation because it doesn't necessarily seem like they're *trying* to be lazy or unhelpful—they just don't get it. They are failing to thrive at work, and many of them don't even realize it.

In working with Know-Nothings, you face several dilemmas:

- How much of your precious time do you spend meeting with them in the hopes that they eventually provide some insights that could be useful?

- How much can you rely on them to get their work done? They are nice enough, which is likely why they are still around, but can you count on them or should you just take it on yourself?

- How much can you ask of them and not seem demanding? While they may not care about their reputation, you care about yours. You don't want their work to affect what you achieve and how you are perceived.

"When we were evaluating a company, it slowly became clear that one of the senior leaders did not really know how the product was made," shared an interviewee who worked in private equity. "He had moved up in the company but was no longer mired in the particulars. He led the team but didn't know the mechanics. My advice? Always know how to do the job of the people below you. Don't micromanage, but understand what is required to get the job done."

Equally perplexing is the notion that Know-Nothings actually do know something, but they are playing coy. Again, you wonder, "Should I keep them close in the hopes they will ultimately reveal themselves?" You need to be mindful that Know-Nothings may know more than they let on or they may be privy to information that they don't even know is useful.

I firmly believe that everyone has value to contribute—sometimes you just need to work a little harder to figure out what that is. The Know-Nothing may initially present as that slap-happy buffoon who knows everyone in the company but doesn't seem to offer much. But here's the thing: more often than not the Know-Nothing knows a lot of people in the company, is familiar with many of the clients, and has been there for a while. There's a lot of historical knowledge in that Know-Nothing brain. Historical knowledge can be amazingly useful to you and even save you time and money.

One interviewee shared his amusement when he uncovered that a Know-Nothing actually knew quite a lot. "We had meeting after meeting with the other company to get educated on their product portfolio. The son or nephew of the former owner was in these meetings. Nice, jovial guy but really didn't seem to have much value to add. After our discussions, we'd determined that there was a new product we could launch fairly inexpensively. It was at this point that he casually chimed in, after asking folks if they wanted coffee, 'Yeah, that type of product line you're suggesting? We pursued that a few years ago and it failed miserably. To make it without compromising our equipment requires super expensive machinery, and getting parts from China is a bureaucratic nightmare.'" Yeah, useful information to know for sure.

Given that the average tenure of salaried workers is a meager 4.2 years[23] at companies these days, having access to someone who has been there for a while can be invaluable. It can save you unnecessary headaches if you have that historical data to add to your collective knowledge.

What's equally interesting is that people tend to share a lot with Know-Nothings. They don't pose a threat, so oftentimes they inadvertently glean a lot of information from colleagues. Information that can be eye-opening for you—and not found in the company's five-year plan.

## When the Know-Nothing actually does know something but intentionally acts stupid

This is delicate because it may take a while to figure that out. If you suspect someone is playing coy and holding back, first try figuring out why. Why would someone be reluctant to share information? Perhaps he thinks it's the only way to hold on to his job. Maybe he's unhappy about the M&A deal and sees no reason to share knowledge. Whatever the reason, it's important to figure out the root cause. Then determine if other people have the same information and seek it out from them. If you can't get the information anywhere else, your best move is to earn the trust of the Know-Nothing who knows something. Check out the chapter "Collaborate with the Other Side" for my best advice on that.

Another interviewee shared that he had an epiphany moment after having drinks with a supposed Know-Nothing: "I liked the guy, so I thought it wouldn't hurt to go have drinks. While chatting I learned that the head of procurement was sleeping with the office manager of another company. While he thought it was simply amusing, I realized it was why the company had a great price deal. Something I hadn't been able to figure out before."

In the spirit of "keep your friends close but your enemies closer," I suggest that when you encounter potential Know-Nothings from the other company, keep your Know-Something's close but your Know-Nothings closer. If you decide to invest the time, they can be a wealth of knowledge. And that's the key—deciding whether the time investment is worth it. There are those who actually don't know anything relevant to you and they aren't really friendly. In that case, I encourage you to move on.

The toughest part of dealing with a Know-Nothing is when that person is your boss. One of my interviewees had this issue, and it was damaging for his entire team. "My boss was a nice guy, but he struggled to connect the dots as the integration was playing out," he said. "Rather than proactively seeking out information, he waited for instructions. This hampered the team's ability to move forward, while other teams went for land grabs ... People chose not to share info with him. That kept him and our team in the dark. Our team eventually went to other people to get their info. When not plugged in, at best you can get left behind, at worst you can get trampled over."

During post-deal M&A integration, having insight into what is going on and why things are happening is critical.

When you are not a source of information, people will *not* go out of their way to keep you informed. You will typically get the general companywide information, but your advantages come from gaining further insight into how and why decisions are being made. This makes you smarter in your own decision-making. You can't afford to become a Know-Nothing yourself. You need to seek out information.

In summary, it will help you to keep these three things in mind regarding Know-Nothings:

1. **Know-Nothings always know something.** Spend the time to find out what it is.

2. **Know-Nothings may not grasp that what they know is useful.** It's up to you to ask the right questions to gather that intel.

3. **You cannot afford to become a Know-Nothing.** Actively seek out information that can help you connect the dots and inform your decisions and your team's actions. And more importantly, the more information you have and share, the more others will share with you.

CHAPTER 13

# The Black Widow

Of all the characters that emerge in the post-deal environment, the Black Widow can be the most lethal. These people present as allies, and that's what you consider them to be. It might be someone you worked with at your original company, someone you thought of as a friend, or a person you could trust. Or it might be someone you got to know from the other company at the beginning of the integration, someone you grew to consider a new ally, seemingly sharing the same values and goals—or so you thought. In the end, it is revealed they didn't value you at all—they just used you to achieve their own ends. Just like the venomous spider known for her tendency to eat her mate, Black Widows move on to the next prey once they've gotten what they need from you.

In your defense, Black Widows want you to believe that they are allies. They will commiserate with you about the nastiness and lunacy of the acquisition. They will bemoan the meetings you each are required to attend, the number of times the strategy changes, and how many hours you are both working on things that make no strategic sense. And you will continue to be open with them about what you are doing, how you are progressing, and ideas you have about how to fix certain issues. They will act fascinated by what you are doing, asking you all sorts of questions, which you will gladly answer without hesitation because you see them as confidantes.

People might tell you to be careful, that they have heard things about these Black Widows. "When trying to figure out who the enemy is, you will usually get warning signs from others; people will tell you be careful, that a guy is not to be trusted," shared one interviewee.

You choose to ignore those warnings. Perhaps they're mistaken. Besides, you'd never fall for that. For crying out loud—you're allies! You are winning this battle together. And then suddenly things change. It starts to dawn on you that perhaps this alliance is not what you thought. Meetings you both were previously invited to, now only he is. When you inquire, you are told that there was not much discussed related to your area and what was, he covered. You are becoming replaceable, expendable, and now your replacement has all the knowledge he needs, because you have been sharing it. You gulp hard with the realization you have fallen prey to the Black Widow!

"Oh yeah, I had a colleague who did me in," revealed an interviewee who'd been VP of Marketing at an acquired security company. "She was my sales counterpart at our company who had allied with me through the integration. I believed we were allies but slowly realized that she felt threatened. She didn't want sales appearing as if they hadn't achieved everything themselves. She positioned me and my marketing team not as an equal but as just a contributor to sales. She not only threw us under the bus, but she backed up over us. It was a hard reality to accept once I understood what had happened."

So how can you tell if you are dealing with a Black Widow, particularly if the person appears to be your ally at a time where you need allies? I don't want to say, "Don't trust anyone!" But I kind of do want to say, "Don't trust anyone—initially." This is not to make you paranoid, but as I keep saying, fear and insecurity change people. And the post-deal work environment breeds these negative tendencies. Be mindful and don't ignore advice to watch out for certain people.

Study the Black Widow's playbook. While I'd promote Dale Carnegie's *How to Make Friends and Influence People* as a preferred playbook (see the Collaboration chapter), the Black Widow prefers Machiavelli's *The Prince* and Robert Greene's *The 48 Laws of Power*. Let's just analyze for a minute what these books are about so you get my meaning.

In *The Prince,* published in 1513, Machiavelli outlined his vision of an ideal leader: an amoral, calculating tyrant for whom the end justifies the means. Specifically, Machiavelli tells his reader to be ruthless in the pursuit of power; that it is better to be feared than to be loved. While the book didn't have the intended effect (he wanted to get back in the good graces of the Medici family—didn't happen), it established Machiavelli as the "father of modern political theory" and *The Prince* as a playbook on how to gain power—ruthlessly.

Robert Greene's *The 48 Laws of Power* was published in 1998. It provides a more contemporary view on gaining power: be cunning. (It is worth noting he also wrote *The Art of*

*Seduction* and *The 33 Strategies of War*). While Greene shares 48 laws, I've pulled the three most relevant and applied them to an M&A situation to reveal the Black Widow's playbook. These should provide insight into how they play the game and how to protect yourself from becoming their prey:

1. **Conceal your intentions**

   *Never show your intentions. Show fake intentions for the purpose of pointing people in the wrong direction. Never allow anyone to see what you really desire.*

   Black Widows hide their intentions. They do this in one of two ways: they don't reveal key information that would give away what they are trying to do, or they talk endlessly about their desires and goals—which are false. They aren't sharing their real intentions but using that "openness" as a way to draw you in.

   Check the intentions of Black Widows against your own. If it seems too good to be true, it usually is. If their stated intentions sound similar to yours, tread carefully. They may have very different intentions but show alignment to gather intelligence. I worked with a Black Widow once, someone I trusted as an ally. We worked on a presentation together and I believed we were aligned on intentions. When it came time to present, she was asked to do the presentation to leadership, not me. Turns out, she had been positioning herself as the leader of the strategy, with me in a secondary role. Ouch.

## 2. Always say less than necessary

*You never learn while you speak. Stay silent and make others speak their plan. Create a sense of false security and use the information acquired to your advantage. Powerful people impress and intimidate by saying less.*

When working with someone you consider an ally, if you find yourself doing most of the talking, be cautious. If when you ask questions they answer vaguely, be hyper cautious. You are likely being used by a Black Widow for the information you have.

After the deal, the temptation to speak up and prove your worth will be strong. Yet in the post-deal landscape, it's a game of appearances, and you don't want to appear too eager. You want people to be aware of your expertise, so keep to what is necessary to share. Not only can you appear more powerful, but Black Widows can't gather your information. Get them to show their cards first. Once the words are out, you cannot take them back.

## 3. Pose as a friend, work as a spy

*Knowing about your rival is critical. Gather information to keep ahead. Ask indirect questions to get people to reveal their weaknesses. Every occasion is a chance to spy.*

You may find yourself in situations where suddenly a lot of people are asking about something you are working on. At first you may be flattered because you believe they are genuinely interested. But over time it may become clear that the information is being shared with someone else, someone you may have considered an ally.

For instance, perhaps you are in a meeting together and when asked a question about the project you are working on, the Black Widow answers it. You wonder, "How could she know? Why did she answer?" Remember the people who've been showing interest? That's how she knows. Why did she answer? Because she's deemed the project important and wants to be aligned with it.

Does this mean you can't trust anyone who appears interested in your projects? No, it doesn't. It simply means be on the alert if suddenly there is a lot of interest in something you are working on. People like to be associated with success, and Black Widows may quickly determine that being attached to you makes them look good. Be open to interested parties but don't over share.[24]

Black Widows believe that the key to power is the ability to judge who is best able to further their interests in all situations. But they can overplay their hand, especially if they present themselves as knowing more than they do. That interviewee who confessed he was done-in by a Black Widow? Turns out she got in over her head. She had presented sales as being able to do it all, but she was not a marketer and could not compensate for that. She was eventually undone as sales declined.

Black Widows are undone eventually, but you can get

caught in their web in the beginning. Be aware of people's intentions, learn their motives, and pay close attention to actions. The more you know about the Black Widows' playbook, the greater chance you have of not getting caught in their web.

YORK

# The Missing-in-Action (MIA)

I feel confident stating that 95% of you have been on at least one multi-person conference call during the course of your career. Whether you are working for a mid-size or multibillion-dollar company, after an acquisition, you will experience an extraordinary number of conference calls. If you think you had a lot before, brace yourself. It is going to quadruple. One of the ways you can identify the Missing-In-Action (MIA) character is through these conference calls.

While trying to integrate efforts, you're often not sure who needs to be on what calls, so *everybody* possibly linked to a project will seem to be invited. I experienced global calls that easily had upwards of 15 people from all over the world, keeping them up at all hours of the night and day. In traditional fashion, people announce themselves at the beginning of the call: "Hi, this is Lars from Denmark." "Sara here." "Jennifer's on." "Hola, this is Miguel." You get the picture.

But our MIA? He doesn't announce himself. In fact, it is not until the end of the call, when you are all signing off, that you even hear his voice. And he may not even say his name—you just hear a meek "Thanks" or a possible "Bye from Bob." And as you hang up you think, "Holy Moses—Bob was on the call? What the heck is Bob doing these days?" And nobody knows. Seriously—no one can clearly articulate what Bob is doing. You wonder how he knew about the call in the first place. You weren't even sure he was still with the company.

Though MIA has military origins[25] it is also used to simply describe someone or something unexpectedly absent or inactive. At work, MIA characters are people who have not been seen in action for quite some time. That's because they selectively decide to participate. They typically don't volunteer or lead. That's why they don't announce themselves at the beginning of those conference calls. They might be asked to volunteer or lead something!

Perhaps they had a job in your earlier company, and even then you were not sure what they did. They may have joined to do a specific task years ago, but that project may have died, launched, or stalled. Whatever its fate, they're still around. They have managed magnificently to work the system and hold a job with no one quite knowing what they do.

"I could never quite understand what exactly her contributions were, even in our old company," shared one interviewee. "We were partnered on a few projects, but she contributed little, always highlighting other projects she was working on. After the merger, I was surprised to see her in meetings. She didn't take ownership of anything, just contributed enough information to show she knew things. It was fascinating to watch."

The fascinating aspect of MIA characters is that people just don't think about them. They can be on calls or in meetings to demonstrate that they do know things, and you can have multiple conversations with them, but they never lead or take ownership of a project. During the confusion of "who does what and who's in charge?" that typically ensues post deal, MIAs can take advantage of that situation.

"I saw *so* many people who just phoned it in after the deal was announced," revealed one interviewee who was part of a multibillion-dollar merger of publications. "They were waiting to see how things played out and just hung on, trying to read the tea leaves, waiting for the payout. I get it, but at the same time it was frustrating because we still had clients to serve."

As tempting as it may be to go MIA during a merger or an acquisition, waiting to see how things play out—that is, not volunteering to lead anything or actively contributing to a project—is a risky move. Those who go MIA do so at their own peril.

"I knew a guy who played MIA really well," shared one interviewee. "No one on the team knew ... who was leading the group, so they were not held accountable. This guy 'snuck out' and went to India while still drawing a paycheck." He added, "But it did catch up with him. Since he was waiting to see who his new boss would be, he didn't really do anything. He provided no value while waiting and had nothing to show for months of work."

So why would someone go MIA at work? In my interviews, I heard everything from "sheer laziness" to "fear of commitment" to "bitterness over the deal." One answer provided helpful perspective: "Some people just don't like to lead. They don't want to be held accountable. They contribute the bare minimum to hold the job but don't want to do more for fear of increasing expectations."

In the grand scheme of things, the MIA is a harmless character. But a lot of MIAs, especially post deal, a time in which you already see a drop in productivity, can cripple a deal's success. You need only look at Gallup's yearly employee engagement survey[26] to see that a lot of disengaged employees can be a problem.

Should your boss go MIA post deal, experience shows that she's likely looking for another job. You might take this to mean you should jump ship too, but that isn't necessarily true. There may be opportunities for you as positions shift and change, which is something I cover in detail in the next section.

If you have colleagues who go MIA after the deal, there are a couple of ways to handle it, depending on whether you've worked with them before or they are new colleagues from the other company. If you've worked with them and what they do is important to your efforts, there are a few ways to draw them out.

1. **Give them recognition.** Nothing tends to motivate people more than being recognized and acknowledged for the work they do, and it's possible that MIAs never had their work recognized. Use this transition period to recognize their work, noting how important it is to the overall

mission and where you are going.

2. **Foster collaboration**. I'm not suggesting you waste energy on someone who is perpetually MIA, but if you see old colleagues retreating during this "in-between" stage right after a deal has gone through, you can help them become re-engaged. It's worth a shot, especially if it can help you (and them) find new purpose at work.

When new colleagues go MIA from the other company, it can get more complicated. "I called these guys the 'non-responsives,'" shared one interviewee. "These are the people you are supposed to be partnering with, who have answers to your questions or who need to partner with you on projects, but they *never* respond. Or if they do, it is delayed by weeks."

These new colleagues may not feel it is necessary to respond because they don't know what you do. There can be so many names in a new organization that people don't know who you are, your value, or your role. To foster collaboration with these colleagues, demonstrate your value and the benefit of partnering together. Actively try to get a face-to-face meeting with anyone you will be expected to work with. It's easy for MIAs to hide when you are just a voice on a phone or an email, even if a persistent one. Demonstrate your value in person as soon as you can.

It can be tempting to go MIA. To "check out" during the transition period to see how the chips fall. This is especially true when no one is really monitoring your activities. But rather than go MIA, I encourage you to make the most of the situation. Identify opportunities that capitalize on what you do but also give you an opportunity to do what you really want. Employees who become disengaged typically do so because they don't find joy in what they do. During this time of transition, create the role that brings you joy.

# 15

# The Specialist

Specialists are those who concentrate primarily on a particular subject or activity and are highly informed in that specific area. They are the company's "go-to" people for that information because they understand it better than anyone else. For example, maybe they are in customer marketing, where you have teams specialized by client industry. They can be research analysts, data scientists, or market trends forecasters. Or they could be part of a specialist team, such as the engineering team, and within that be specialized even further. The key is that for Specialists, their success and value come from having depth of expertise in one area.

Specialists can also be found at any level of the organization. You might have a Head of Digital Marketing (yes, that used to be specialized) or maybe a Chief Technology Officer who is the organization's guru on technology topics. These Specialists' skills and knowledge were integral to your original company's mission and objectives. They were critical because their knowledge helped support or even drive the company's business goals. The tough part after a merger or acquisition is knowing whether or not that expertise will remain valued and important.

There's long raged a debate whether it's better to be a Specialist or a Generalist. Unlike a Specialist's depth of expertise in an area, a Generalist has a broad range of knowledge across the business. Both roles have merit and value, and determining which role is more important really does depend on the business and the situation. Though the debate continues, with the pace of change it would seem Specialists have had the upper hand as companies seek talent highly skilled in certain areas.[27] Which is great when you have that skillset, but as technology continues to advance, those skills can become obsolete or less valued sooner than anticipated. Remember when being a digital guru was a coveted expertise? Now your kids are digital gurus.

Knowing whether or not their expertise will remain valued can gnaw at Specialists. Will their expertise be relevant as the company merges with another and aggressively explores a new market or industry? Can they stay important if their expertise is automotive and the company is pushing into telecommunications? Will the new acquisition and drive for efficiencies through Artificial Intelligence eliminate their role (though this paranoia is not exclusive to Specialists)? Will the unique knowledge they hold still be as valued as it once was? These types of questions can understandably distress Specialists, who have built up solid reputations as experts.

If you work with Specialists or manage them, they will likely try to figure out their value in the future landscape by continuously asking others whether or not they think their role will still be relevant. The tough part is you can't always be certain at the beginning. On the one hand, you think their expertise was important to what you did before, so how could that change? But then you hear that the new company will pursue a direction in a completely new industry. You just don't know if they will still be valued in the same way.

A sales leader I interviewed offered helpful insight on solving this dilemma. He shared a story regarding a customer-marketing manager who was worried about her role post deal. "She'd been a strong analyst on the automotive industry, and we were shifting focus toward mobile," he told me. "I emphasized that regardless of our direction, we still needed to advise on industries that would influence our business strategy long term. I equally reinforced that her success moving forward relied less on what industry she was an expert on and more on how quickly she got smart on an industry. She needed to demonstrate her capacity to learn quickly."

In a post-M&A deal environment, you will be evaluated on your ability to get up to speed rapidly. When speed of execution is critical, no one wants to pay you to learn.[28] A Specialist typically has already demonstrated a strong capacity to learn a topic by the very nature of their role. They need to reinforce this skillset post deal.

Specialists are very proud of their unique knowledge, so it can be difficult not to make their value all about their depth of expertise in a single subject. Specialists therefore face a dilemma: not knowing whether their expertise will be as critical post deal, do they become known within the new company as *the* expert in a particular area and hope that this expertise will remain relevant? Or do they recast themselves to align with the new vision?

Here is when being smart *and* patient becomes valuable and may allow you to have your cake and eat it too.

"We waited for months to learn if our deal was going through," shared an interviewee. "We didn't know which company would lead if the deal went through. My specialty team was convinced that their expertise wouldn't be valued post deal. I suggested they stay focused on being good at their jobs while identifying how that knowledge would be valuable post deal. It paid off. Once the deal went through, even though the other company took the lead, my team quickly demonstrated how their expertise could contribute to the future vision."

Specialists do need to be willing to evolve when their expertise becomes a commodity or obsolete. As I shared earlier in the Stages of Grief section, during the M&A deal integration phase, companies experience a neutral zone[29] in which they slowly let go of the old ways but have not yet adapted the new. If you are a Specialist, this period can be a great opportunity to see how your skills can be of value to the new way of doing things and then demonstrate how that knowledge or expertise will play a role in the future vision. The key is being willing to evolve when your expertise becomes a commodity or obsolete.

Patience can be hard when you want to know what your value will be post deal. The reality is that increased automation, the fixation on big data, and the dawn of artificial intelligence has changed everything for everyone. No one is immune to these influential factors. So, don't get pigeonholed. In today's world, no one can afford to become complacent. You are the person in control of that; make sure it doesn't happen. Branch out and make sure you know others in the company and that they know you, not just for the deep expertise you have but your ability to learn quickly and contribute expertise. The integration's success is going to rest on people like you.

# CHAPTER 16

# The Opportunist

Meet the Opportunist. He thinks you're incredibly smart, talented, full of great ideas, and truly an inspiration to both the company and society at large. Now, what can you do to help him?

If we all had to vote on which personality type is the most annoying, the Opportunist would likely get high marks due to lack of authenticity. This personality type has also been called a suck-up, a brown-noser, an apple polisher, or even the Shakespearean-sounding sycophant.

Opportunists are those people you observe constantly offering praise to whomever they think has power or can do something for them. You will hear them offering excessive compliments in order to gain that person's favor.

Similar to the other characters, Opportunists exist even before an M&A deal. Yet they can emerge more dramatically post acquisition as they begin to feel insecure about their role. When people are operating out of fear, the operative post-deal emotion, they quickly try to assess what will be required to survive. This is the "fight or flight" reaction. Opportunists assess the situation and determine that their survival relies on impressing the people in power who have potential control over their future.

Right after a deal goes through, there are many unknowns: Do I still have a job? What will my role be? Will my team be valued? People understandably get anxious. One way they try to answer these questions is by warming up to as many people as possible. When someone you've seen in passing for years starts being friendly to you for the first time, you might be seeing the Opportunist emerge. Remember, fear brings out a whole new side of people. This is not to judge the behavior good or bad. It's simply a result of that person switching to survivor mode.

"At the beginning days of an acquisition, this one guy would practically fall all over our leader to curry his favor. It was almost to the point of being embarrassing," shared one of my interviewees. "I suspected that he was in over his head and thought the best way to distract from that was to do whatever our boss asked."

As a witness to all of this, you may be perpetually amused by Opportunists' actions. You wonder if they realize how obvious they are, since fawning can take on outsized proportions. ("Joe, I saved you a seat right up front for the presentation. And here's a cup of coffee, just the way you like it!")

Equally interesting is that Opportunists' allegiances can shift as they re-evaluate who is truly in power. One day, they may be all over Joe, but a week later, they could shift to someone who seems to have more power. Joe may even suddenly get the cold shoulder. Since Opportunists' motives and actions are usually fairly obvious to everyone else but them, it can be amusing to watch.

"I was the recipient of a lot of adulation at the beginning of one acquisition," shared a VP whose company conducted several acquisitions. "I shared with the new team that what impressed me most was what they had achieved to date and how they saw their skills contributing to the future. I wanted to make it abundantly clear that I was looking for people with expertise—not 'yes' men or women."

In today's competitive world, where it feels like your status is the most important thing, it can be tempting to hold on to your job and stature by ingratiating yourself to your new boss or anyone else you think could be in charge of your future. This is a short-sighted strategy. Your best path to success is to demonstrate your smarts. Trying to succeed simply by complimenting others is a strategy that will ultimately work against you.

Instead of brown nosing, keep earning your job. Command respect through your work and actions. People may enjoy the flattery, but that won't earn you their respect. A constant dose of it, and people can see right through it. Even if you actually do receive something that you covet from all your fawning, the person you fawned all over will forever see you as subservient, not as an equal or as someone with future potential. It takes the focus off your actual value and compromises your integrity. People will wonder if you don't value yourself, what do you value?

One interviewee in the energy industry watched firsthand as an admired colleague groveled and lost his way after their company was acquired: "I worked with this really smart guy who desperately wanted to be accepted as part of the leadership 'boys' club' ... but he had been passed by many times for promotion. He became a suck-up to get to that next level, but it worked against him. His new boss just used him and relied on him less and less as the perception of his value diminished. It was hard to watch."

This is *not* to say that everyone who flatters people is a suck-up. You will see in my later chapter on collaborating with the other side that one of the best ways to foster collaboration, as posited by none other than Dale Carnegie, is to actively make those meetings with new co-workers about *them*. Learn about them and ask questions to build trust. If you do this the wrong way, could you come across as an Opportunist? Possibly.

So how do you use flattery in a way that helps you connect with a boss or leader without labelling you as an Opportunist? Here are three different approaches I love, conducted by researchers from Northwestern University and the University of Michigan, identifying several powerful tactics for gaining social influence without coming across as a suck-up. The study drew from theory and research on interpersonal attraction, as well as interviews with 42 managers and CEOs, and identified effective forms of ingratiation most likely to help executives win board seats.

1. **Frame flattery as advice seeking**: "How were you able to get the product team to move up their launch date?"

2. **Argue or show doubt prior to conforming**: "At first, I didn't see your point, but it makes total sense now. You've convinced me."

3. **Engage in "value conformity" prior to flattery, to show you agree on a deep level**: "I'm

the same way. I believe we should have Marketing reporting to Sales."[30]

You might feel that even these examples sound a bit "suck-up-y." It all depends on how much you use flattery to build a relationship. Don't just *show* interest—*have* genuine interest. If you rely purely on flattery as a way to connect, yes, that smacks of being an Opportunist. If you want to learn more about your boss or colleague to connect and work better together, find out about their life, their family, and their interests. That's how to build a relationship—well beyond what a frequent dose of flattery can.

Finally, assume the best of others, and if you feel that someone is being excessively complimentary, try to determine why that might be. Are they trying to save their job and see you as the ticket? Is there a role on your team they are seeking to secure? Consider the reasoning. Also recognize that we have *all* likely played this role at some point in our career. We like to think that we are above this type of behavior and quick to observe it in others, but there is a pretty good chance we've done it as well. In the early stages, expect that there will be lots of Opportunists post deal. The key will be to quickly identify what is needed for success and then demonstrate your ability to contribute. Know and show your value.

# 17

# The Ostrich

If someone accuses you of being an Ostrich, it essentially means you are refusing to confront or acknowledge a situation. "Don't bury your head in the sand like an Ostrich," comes from the supposed habit of ostriches hiding when faced with their predators. The notion being that the dumb ostrich believes that if it can't see its attacker then the attacker can't see it.[31] The Ostrich character is firmly in denial.

While aspects of this character reveal a tendency to hide from the realities of a post-acquisition world, this personality is not to be confused with the Missing-In-Action personality. Ostriches are clear on what their contributions to the company have been, but they have a difficult time accepting the changes they see happening and understanding how they can still contribute. They essentially "stick their head in the sand" in the hopes that the change will simply go away. Their philosophy is, "If I just ignore it, this change won't happen. Give it time, and things will go back to the way they were."

Being in denial about change happening around you is

understandable. As described in its own chapter, denial is a coping mechanism. It gives your brain time to adjust to distressing situations, like the post-M&A environment. The issue for Ostriches is that they stay in denial. They use denial to protect themselves and refuse to accept the truth about what is happening.

They are proud of their skills and were likely well known for their past accomplishments, so they have a difficult time seeing how their skills can contribute or be leveraged in the future—to the point where they become almost paralyzed. In fact, when people tell Ostriches that their skills could be valuable in the new company, they can be resistant.

"A work colleague I knew was definitely an Ostrich, which was a shame," shared an interviewee who experienced a mid-sized company merger. "She had been an office manager and proud of her work. When the merger took place, she couldn't understand why. She felt it somehow meant her job was no longer valued. That she was no longer valued. Her work could have remained valued if she'd evolved, but she stayed stuck in denial hoping everything would just go back to the way it was."

According to research by the Mayo Clinic, people in denial do the following:[32]

- Won't acknowledge a difficult situation
- Try not to face the facts of a problem
- Downplay possible consequences of the issue

These are the tell-tale signs of an Ostrich. These people typically were quite proud of the work they did, so the news of a merger or acquisition with another company can present a new reality they have a hard time adjusting to. They go into the denial stage because this news threatens their sense of control. Denial can only be a temporary measure—it won't change the reality of the situation—and the Ostrich has a hard time seeing this.

So how do you help Ostriches? First and foremost be patient, especially if they are people you have enjoyed working with, who could be great contributors in the future if they just take a little time to adjust. Demanding they "face the facts and move on" will only antagonize them and likely push their heads down further into the proverbial sand. They might just need a little time to accept the new reality. Let them know that you are open to talking about the changes and are happy to be a sounding board. Listen and offer support.

If the Ostrich happens to be your boss, honestly, you can only help so much. When people are in denial and ignoring what's happening around them, they are likely to only last so long.

Now for the tough question: What if the Ostrich is you? Frankly, the majority of people play the Ostrich role for a bit because being in denial about potentially disruptive or unexpected news is the first stage of grief. Almost everyone experiences it. But a full-fledged Ostrich stays in denial too long. If you find that you are having a hard time facing reality, that you are ignoring the changes happening around you and fixating on how you have always done things, then you are likely exhibiting Ostrich traits. If people are increasingly saying things to you like, "Yes, I know that's how it used to work, but we need to evolve how we do things as we integrate with this new company," then you are likely being seen as a bit of an Ostrich.

Here are three ways to help you get out of your Ostrich mindset:

1.  **Ask yourself what you are afraid of.** Is it loss of control? Is it the fear your job is no longer important? That you won't be able to adapt to this new company? Examine what you fear and identify any possibly irrational beliefs about your new situation. Articulating these fears helps you begin to address them and adapt.

2.  **Consider the consequences of not taking action.** Being an Ostrich can hurt your efforts as others adapt around you. You need to be honest with yourself and consider what could happen if others evolve while you don't.

3.  **Find a trusted friend outside of work to open up to.** Allow yourself to express your fears and emotions, acknowledging the potential negative consequences of not adapting. Talking these issues through will help you to see a way forward.[33]

It's okay to say, "I just can't think about this right now." But denial can only be a temporary response; it won't change the reality of the new situation. It is imperative that you accept that change is happening—that it has happened—and your opportunity lies in figuring out how your skillset contributes to the new future.

CHAPTER

# 18

# The Dominatrix

In any business transformation, you need leaders who will plow forward to make things happen, especially when certain changes aren't popular. The Dominatrix doesn't overanalyze people's feelings or work to build consensus. These individuals concentrate on the business objectives with laser-like focus and they work to get them done.

Without this kind of character, organizations would be at a standstill. And given the sense of urgency wrapped around most M&A deals, the Dominatrix is perfect for driving quick results that key stakeholders want post deal. Dominatrices certainly add value, but they have a downfall: they lack people skills. And in many cases, that would be putting it lightly.

Dominatrices can be considered ruthless. They simply do not value other people's emotions the same as the rest of us. They are prepared to do whatever it takes to achieve their goals, and sometimes it can get nasty. They gain their power by bullying, dominating, or manipulating others. And they don't really attempt to hide these tendencies (unlike the Black Widow, who you met earlier) because they are not concerned with what their plebian coworkers think of them. Finally, keep in mind that bullying and dominating tendencies show up in *all genders*.

In most cases, Dominatrices enjoy flaunting their bad behaviors. It is part of how they gain their position—making sure everyone understands that it's their way or the highway. They have no qualms about employing sly tactics to do what needs to be done. In their mind, all actions are justified because it's for the good of the company. Their rabid focus on the business objectives can help them move up the corporate ladder, becoming a critical player in an organization's success.

Their work style doesn't make them very many friends along the way, but the truth is, they aren't trying to make friends. They're about execution and end results. Whoever is left standing next to them when those are achieved doesn't really matter; they're already on to the next task. This dominating tendency makes them a force to be reckoned with in any organization that needs to get things done—which, let's face it, is pretty much every organization today.

Dominatrices can take things way too far by going on a power trip where their actions don't actually benefit the company. This is when things can really go sour. "The Dominatrix I worked with had been at the company for a while and had a lot of product knowledge. Her career had stagnated because she rubbed several leaders the wrong way. Once we were acquired, she morphed into a Dominatrix," shared one interviewee. "She leveraged her product insights for her betterment and insinuated herself with new leadership to get plum responsibilities. She insisted

# The five telling signs you are working with a Dominatrix

1. **Risk taking and a willingness to push things ahead.**

   Where others might hesitate, say push to gather more data or wait for group consensus, the Dominatrix will charge forward and become easily annoyed by any handwringing from others.

2. **Charms people into following them.**

   Through their inspiring oratory skills and confident presentation, they often can convince people that their way is the only way forward.

3. **Tendency toward grandiosity, with big schemes and plans.**

   These bosses thrive on an amazing array of complicated spreadsheets and detailed PowerPoint slides (which are put together by someone else) that paint a vivid picture of how the plan or strategy is so obvious and must be pursued.

4. **Indifference to other people's opinions.**

   Remember, they are tasked with "getting it done." They don't have time to debate.

5. **Mistrusting of others and believing those who disagree are the enemy.**

   Given their view that others don't get the bigger picture, anyone who questions the plan or isn't "all in" is a target for their wrath.

her team lead projects even when they were not the most qualified. She overpowered people in meetings and cut them off because she knew enough about the products not to care." The interviewee concluded, "The hardest part was that we had all worked together. She turned other people on her team combative toward our team so they could keep control. She set that example and her team followed suit."

Many of my interviewees highlighted the Dominatrix as a forceful character who had good and bad traits, who could make great progress quickly in an organization but be absolutely destructive to morale in getting there. They equally noted the unique leadership styles of Dominatrices. They could be either a seductress or a straight-out bully, depending on what tactic helped them achieve their objectives. They acted differently depending on the audience and their needs.

When dealing with Dominatrices in M&A, remember they've been appointed the designated "enforcer," tasked with the dirty work of pushing through the acquisition and the integration. If you are having trouble with this, you need to consider the role you want to play in the change. If you believe in the change yet have reservations about some of the decisions and how they will be executed, you need to present those concerns in a rationalized way versus as an emotional challenge. A Dominatrix has no time for emotionally driven pushback. If you present your concerns as supportive of the change but demonstrate the practical challenges you/the team could face in executing them, a Dominatrix will see you not as a threat but as a valuable player.

Several of my interviewees shared helpful perspectives and lessons learned while working with the Dominatrix. The key is to know your value. Be confident in your skills and show how your experience will contribute to the change and the Dominatrix's vision of how it should happen. If you don't doubt your skills, the Dominatrix should have no reason to either. Consider this advice to navigate the various situations you may face:

1. **Know more about something than they do (or ever could).**

   Become invaluable by being an expert on something critical to their vision. Make sure they are aware of your expertise. Make yourself essential to their success.

   Example: *"I have been digging into the latest budget forecasting and I think there is a way to shave costs in product development so that we can fund the new project you identified as critical. If you'd like I could crunch the numbers and come back to you with ways we might do this."*

2. **Never doubt them (openly).**

   Do not express negative feelings about something they have said or proposed in an open forum. If you do, your goose is cooked. While you may have good reason to doubt or question what's proposed, you need to be smart about how you engage. When asking a question, phrase it in a way that highlights their brilliance.

   Example: *"I am really intrigued by the business strategy you shared for the department. I see a role for our team in helping to achieve your vision, but I would benefit from further discussion to make sure my thinking is aligned with yours. Would you have time to meet and help me understand how we can contribute to the objectives you defined?"*

### 3. Consistently provide valuable intel.

Be smart on the data: what you have, what the gaps in knowledge are, questions that remain, etc. The more intelligence you have that informs the vision being pursued, the more valuable you will be. One caution: people will clam up quickly if they think you're leveraging the data to serve your own agenda. Provide insightful perspective without being a brownnoser (read the Opportunist for advice on that).

Example: *"I know in the last meeting there was concern your proposal might be too ambitious, but I am hearing from the product guys that we could actually make that timeline work. We would just need to eliminate one of the approval stages that really is unnecessary for this type of plan. It might be worth following up on."*

### 4. Compliment them.

Praise the vision they have laid out, the strategy they have defined, or the presentations they give. As tough as Dominatrices present themselves, they still react positively to acknowledgment of their efforts. Find the positives and be generous with praise.

Example: *"I found your presentation enormously helpful. How you laid out the future business strategy helped it finally make sense. My team would benefit from having you present your vision directly to them."*

5. **Don't bother trying to get close**.
   When pushing through change, especially unpopular change, it's hard to make friends. Your path to a productive partnership is through demonstrating the value you bring to helping achieve the vision, not in becoming the Dominatrix's BFF.

   Example: *"Hey there, just wanted to say good night. I will have that spreadsheet adjusted with your comments, and on your desk, first thing in the morning."*

My last piece of advice, born from dealing with a few Dominatrices across the course of my three acquisition experiences: more than any other character, Dominatrices have certain triggers that could ruin your ability to work with them and succeed. In the spirit of having a little fun, here are a few quick ways to annoy the hell out of your Dominatrix (meaning, don't do these if you want to succeed):

- Question his judgment
- Ask questions that clearly demonstrate you don't see the bigger picture
- Delay execution because you think others should be engaged or consensus built
- Don't follow-up with him on a request he made

- Quote someone who he clearly despises
- Openly doodle while he is presenting

Dominatrices can play a critical role in the short term but almost always struggle later, as teams are rarely inspired by fear in the long term. Their dominating approach can compel people to stall their efforts, resist the forceful approach, or even leave the company. The question is whether you can weather the storm, thrive during the downpour, and maintain hold on a functioning umbrella. Your ability to manage this character will serve you well throughout your career, as the Dominatrix will definitely not be your last difficult boss.

# SECTION 4

Now What?

# 19

# Have the Right Mindset

After consulting with so many people going through M&A, I've learned some pretty interesting things about how one's headspace can actually make a difference in how one emerges from M&A. So if you have the inclination to breeze through this advice on "soft" skills, I urge you to cool your jets. This chapter will be worth your while.

First and foremost, know that *attitude matters more than just about everything else.* As one of my interviewees shared, "It can even matter more than what degree you have or how good you are at your job." Why? Because when you have a positive approach, people will want to work with you. Think about it—who likes working with a "Negative Nellie?" And in times of M&A, when so much is in flux, so many people are disgruntled and resisting change, and new teams are being formed, having the right attitude is the best way to set yourself apart. People will see that you care and that you're trying your best. That eventually rubs off on others. When the post-deal reality feels complicated and overwhelming, and morale starts to drop, having a positive attitude is such a simple thing to do. And best of all—it is within your control.

If you want to know how to keep your job or get an even better job at your organization, focus on having a positive attitude. I've seen it time and time again. People with positive attitudes get more opportunities than their coworkers. Their positive attitude demonstrates resilience during trying times, and senior leadership is universally impressed by that. And yes, the higher ups *are* watching you. The post-deal environment is like one big, ongoing interview. Everyone is evaluated for what they can contribute. A positive attitude shows new people what you are made of.

Now, having a good attitude is one of those things that is often easier said than done. I recognize that. And having a positive attitude doesn't mean becoming a "yes" person or a suck up (please, dear God, as said in an earlier chapter, do not become one of those). Nor does it mean blindly following orders without the slightest idea of where you're headed. You are not expected to shut up and smile. It's important to keep this in mind, because sometimes people feel like they can't be positive or authentic or contribute anything at all if they don't agree with every single aspect of the post-deal landscape.

As the consummate professional you are, your perspective is valuable. You know how to do things that other people in the organization do not. If you see an issue arising from proposed plans, you should speak up and offer a solution based on your knowledge and expertise. You can still challenge things in a productive way without being obstinate or emotional. This is how you support the new vision.

Don't abdicate your role in helping achieve the new vision, especially as it relates to your job duties. All too often,

## What's best for the customer?

This is my favorite question to ask in any post-deal situation. It eliminates the "us vs. them" thinking, and it helps get off-kilter strategies back on track. When you get in the mindset of always putting your customer first, it becomes a lot easier to make the right decisions. I learned this from an old ad agency boss who shared his experience when Foote, Cone & Belding merged with Draft Worldwide in 2006. One of the key FCB accounts going into the merger was Coors. After the merger, the leadership team wanted to sell a merged portfolio of services to Coors, which included direct mail. My boss knew Coors had a direct mail agency and what they had was better. When the leadership team kept urging him to try to upsell to Coors, he stuck to his guns and said, "Do you want to keep Coors as a customer or lose them?" It was such a simple question, but it hit the nail right on the head. Why would a customer stay, even a loyal one, if decisions being made are not in their best interest?

I've seen experienced professionals fall silent during times of M&A because they don't want to be seen as a problem or are worried about putting a target on their back. Other times, leaders start to question their own knowledge, so they step down from involvement instead of speaking up. This is especially true when a swarm of consultants come in, armed and ready to dictate a new strategy. Even if—dare I say especially if—you're working with some big-wig consulting firm! You have invaluable knowledge that someone coming in from the cold does not have. Keep this in mind to maintain a positive attitude. It ensures you don't lose your sense of purpose or your voice.

## Curb your frustration

We've talked a lot about how people hate change, and that it's unavoidable in M&A. But one thing that can be incredibly frustrating is when things *keep* changing. Sometimes it feels like as soon as you get all the cats herded in one direction, you're told to turn them all around. Over. And over. And over. It's hard not to feel like you've wasted time and energy, and this feeling can be incredibly damaging for morale.

Be mentally prepared for plans to keep changing. Because in all likelihood, they will. When the original post-deal strategy was defined, it likely didn't include the people who know how everything actually runs. When those people get looped in (which includes you by the way) things change. And then when everyone starts doing the work, unexpected complications arise, causing plans to shift again. This is part of the journey. As Dwight D. Eisenhower once said, "Plans are useless, but planning is indispensable." It's best to have plans, backup plans, and backup backup plans. Because when plan A and B fail, instead of being frustrated, you know you have a plan C.

As you continue forward in your M&A journey, try to let things roll off your back instead of getting frustrated. Remember this is a discovery process for everyone, and you're all on this journey together. You don't have all the answers, and neither do your senior leaders. Everyone makes mistakes, and it's important to be tolerant of others. Give people the benefit of the doubt, and don't look to place blame when things don't go as planned. Keep a positive attitude.

When it feels like a dark comedy, find the humor. It's there. Crazy things will happen, and it helps if you can laugh about it. Everyone experiences change differently, but it's universally emotional. If you can bring a light-hearted approach to your work and see the humor in odd moments, it will help you and your colleagues get through these transitions.

CHAPTER 20

# Collaborate with the Other Side

M&A can unlock new opportunities for you, changing your scope of work into something much more interesting and fulfilling. Trust me, it can—even if you don't believe it at first. But to uncover these post-deal career opportunities, first you need to learn about the other company—and that holds whether the M&A deal just went through or is still on the horizon. You want to get as smart as you can about how the other company operates. Then once the deal goes through, you'll want to get to know your new colleagues and how they do business.

M&A is about *bringing together two businesses to create something better.* In describing the ideal union, I use the marriage analogy. Consider the most functional relationships you've seen. The partners can be totally different, but what binds them beyond love is their respect for one another and that they recognize and value their different strengths. Instead of one side trying to force the other into changing, they realize they are stronger together and work to bring out

165

the best in each other. That's how you need to approach this union. I know that sounds easier said than done, especially when you are still reeling from the deal news.

Too often success stalls because people exhibit the "not invented here" syndrome. Instead of embracing new ideas and ways of doing things, people dig in their heels and avoid anything that wasn't invented by them or on their side of the company. Obviously, this is not a way to find common ground, nor will it bring out the best in each other.

A great example of two very different companies coming together and finding common ground is Nordstrom and Trunk Club. I was on an M&A panel with Linda Bartman, COO at Trunk Club, and she emphasized that success comes from being open to what you can learn from each other:

> "Nordstrom looked at Trunk Club and asked, 'How can we gain an understanding of how to move and make decisions quickly and maintain that pace?' Trunk Club looked at Nordstrom and asked, 'How can we get more rigor around our process so that we can make better, more informed decisions?' We even came to meetings with different perspectives because we looked at things very differently. An example is Trunk Club saying, 'We are launching a new product in two weeks!' with Nordstrom wondering, 'You're doing what?!' But that tension can be good and result in better decisions."[34]

Although the acquisition hasn't been entirely without hiccups (and what acquisition is?), the companies have taken the time to appreciate and leverage one another's strengths. This is the cornerstone of collaborating.

When it comes to informal collaboration, the key is showing that you're genuinely interested in getting to know your new colleagues. This is the number-one way to get them to like you, proven by Dale Carnegie in *How to Win Friends and Influence People*. Although written in the 1930s, his advice is evergreen: "You can make more friends in two months by being interested in them, than in two years by making them interested in you."[35]

Ask questions to learn about the other side: What are their client relationships like? Are they marketing, sales, or product driven? Are they hierarchical or entrepreneurial? How do they make decisions? Answering these questions is the starting point, since you'll need knowledge to determine how to best move forward with your work and your team's work.

Even if you're consumed by worries about your own job or what's going to happen with your project, resist bringing these things up when you first meet your new colleagues. Make your first interactions about them. This is how you show you're invested in the good of the organization rather than just your own personal gains.

To get the collaboration ball rolling, you'll want to be proactive. I can't tell you how many times I kick-started the collaboration by making the first move.

- Make the first gesture within a week or two of being introduced to your new colleagues.
- Reach out to a couple of new team members and say you want to get to know them and learn more

about what they do.

- Whenever possible, meet in person. This gives you a much better sense of someone versus talking on the phone.

- Keep it informal—it's hard to resist meetings over lunch or coffee!

The priority of these meetings is about getting to know people. Your job during these meetings is to listen and get to know your new colleagues. Be curious, friendly, and genuinely interested. Trust me, this will lay the foundation for future collaboration.

Listening also encourages people to open up. In the post-deal environment, information is like gold, and a lot of the most interesting and helpful things to know are not printed in the employee handbook or in the five-year strategy documents. You can only get the real scoop from speaking with people directly. Once you get to know your new colleagues and earn their trust, they'll feel comfortable opening up about all kinds of things, such as senior leaders' priorities and work styles, how to impress them, and how to avoid getting on their bad side. You can also gain insight into what's worked for the company in the past, as well as what hasn't gone well, which is information that can help identify opportunities for you. But this information sharing shouldn't be one-sided.

You have to give information to get it. Be forthcoming about information on your side of the company as well. One of my interviewees held a junior role but had unique insights into the company strategy due to her work for one of the executives. "Being an 'information person' helped me earn people's trust," she shared. "Obviously I didn't share confidential information, but I was able to provide context to some of the decisions being made. I found that people felt more comfortable conversing with me because I was junior and that ultimately they reciprocated, sharing all kinds of helpful information with me as well."

In addition to these kinds of informal actions, your company may need to embark on some larger-scale, formal efforts as well. This can be especially helpful when two companies have radically different cultures or ways of getting things done. Jodi Navta was CMO of Coyote when they were acquired by UPS in 2015. Both companies had a lot of success in logistics going into the acquisition, but they got there in different ways. To come together, they needed to create a formal structure for helping employees collaborate. "You could have had one buttoned-up culture (UPS) just looking quizzically at the other jeans and t-shirt-oriented culture (Coyote), but we quickly learned we shared core common values," said Jodi. "We accelerated face-to-face meetings and had people from both sides travel the road together on joint sales calls. It created an almost familial culture where the millennial workers felt proud to teach what they did and vice-versa."[36]

Some of these initiatives will come down from the top, but you might equally find yourself in a perfect position to spearhead your own efforts. If you see the need for greater collaboration and nothing is being done to make it happen, don't be afraid to step up and make a recommendation.

This is especially true when defining decision-making steps as your two companies integrate processes, systems, or procedures. And what a headache this can be! Deciding who makes what decision when can be a pain. You want to be collaborative, but sometimes that turns into having too many cooks in the kitchen. And delayed decision-making can hurt customer outcomes. (Remember this from Section 1 as one of the most common reasons M&A fails.) You can't wait for senior leadership to always know how to redraw the decision-making lines.

An immediate and productive way to collaborate with the other side is to find the right balance of letting people weigh in on decisions without delaying the process, i.e., defining your RACI[37] for who is:

- Responsible
- Accountable
- Consulted
- Informed

Defining roles from the beginning and co-creating the decision-making process cuts back on the number of decision makers, reduces bottlenecks, and has everyone feeling invested in the process. For many companies, this exercise can truly be a Godsend.

## Learn their language to understand their culture

All companies have unique phrases and nomenclature; it's part of their culture. To understand their culture, learn their language. I know of a merger that joined together a company that provided onsite security personnel with a company that provided cyber security. The onsite security company called their employees "security officers," not "security guards." They felt that "officers" better spoke to the level of sophistication of the role. As such, being called security guards rubbed employees the wrong way. The cyber security firm that acquired them did not pick up on this and sent the unintended message that they didn't respect the onsite security company. Long story short: words matter. If you're coming from different industries, or say one is B2B and the other is B2C, each uses a different language. Make sure your side of the company puts in effort to learn the other side's terminology.

As you and your new colleagues have those first forced, awkward interactions, remember that it's difficult on both sides. Don't get caught up in the "us vs them" dynamic, which is a pervasive issue I covered in *Harvard Business Review*[38]. People often think of M&A as "our company" versus "their company." You might even think, "No way am I giving away insider information on our company. They'll turn that information to their advantage!" But remember, their advantage can now be your advantage—with collaboration. Try to keep that in mind. (Besides, I've got a later chapter on politics to keep you smart when it comes to the drama—err, "social dynamics"—of M&A.) Both sides have their own insecurities, issues, and shortcomings. And both sides have their own strengths. That's why you need each other. I'm going to go ahead and say that again: *you need each other.* When things start to feel tough, keep going back to that fact.

CHAPTER 21

# Finding Your Niche

Opportunity is the silver lining to M&A. No matter how uncomfortable (or utterly painful) things have been, you're in the midst of change. That can only mean one thing: there is the opportunity for both your long-term career and your day-to-day reality to get much, much better. But let's be clear: It's an *opportunity*, not a surefire thing. You're unlikely to be handed anything on a silver platter. That said, you absolutely have the ability to guide your future at your organization. But you need to be strategic about it. Now is your chance to define what you want your future role to look like and figure out how to get there.

This comes with a paradox: You need to keep doing your current job well while defining the job you want in the new organization. Let's talk first about your current role.

Given all the changes and uncertainty, it's easy to get distracted from doing your job. Don't let this happen. Even if you believe your job is going to change, or some of your tasks are going to become obsolete, keep doing your job until someone in charge tells you to stop. This will help you stick out in the chaos as someone who is professional, reliable, and can handle change. Some of your colleagues will seem like they're lost at sea. Your ability to stay focused gives you a leg up, and that's important because leadership is looking to see who can keep their cool. Once you're going through an integration, you're basically also going through an ongoing job interview. What people think about you matters, and it can greatly affect your future. So even if your current responsibilities are "sunsetting" (as they like to say in business instead of the harsher "being eliminated"), leaders will be more confident in you if you have continued to do great work. I have seen this time and time again at companies in a range of industries. Even if your company has thousands of people, you can stand out in the post-deal environment by continuing to do your job well.

As you continue being a Rock Star in your current role, you also need to think about what's next. There are a lot of moving pieces and a lot of work to be done, and you need to figure out how you want to fit into this changing landscape. In every M&A deal, there is always additional work that needs to be done. Some of this work is temporary and will help get the new company up to speed, and some of the work will be ongoing. There will also be opportunities from newly vacated positions, as colleagues shift into different roles, find jobs elsewhere, or are let go. Below are a few strategies to keep in mind.

## Make your interests known

Now is the time to pursue your interests. Your boss and other senior leaders are not mind readers. Even if you've made some remarks over the years about how you would like to do more XYZ, there's a good chance they don't remember, or that it's not top-of-mind as they continue to fight for their own jobs. If you have a new boss, he or she will have no clue. Start by talking with your boss to ask whether he or she sees any opportunities for you to go down a different path. This could be within your own department or a new one.

Having casual, informal conversations with your colleagues and key influencers is also a good idea. Showing interest in other aspects of your company is a positive thing, so don't be shy. So much is changing at the organization, this is the perfect time to pivot into a role that better aligns with your skills, interests, and passions.

## Be your own advocate

I'm going to be straight: Your boss may or may not be fighting for you. There are a lot of things competing for everyone's attention right now, and the only person you can rely on is you. That's why it is essential that you actively manage your reputation and image, otherwise known as your personal brand. People at your company need to know what you do. And if you work with clients, they should know too. The more you are known for the value you bring, the better your shot at staying and getting the role you want. This is not the time to go MIA (re-read that chapter if you forgot why).

Make sure you are always prepared to speak to your value internally. If you find yourself in an unexpected conversation with a key influencer, you don't want to waste the opportunity. You always want to position your value around relevant skills and experience, rather than tying it to your current role. People see you as an asset rather than someone whose skillset is limited to his or her current position. This is especially important if you get the sense that your current role isn't valued as much by the new company. You want to proactively show how your skills could fit another role.

Remember, you are on a continual job interview early in the post-integration phase, so approach interactions as you would an interview. I recommend using the CARS method when describing what you have achieved: describe the Challenge, the Action you took, the Results you saw, and finally, the Skills you gained.[39] When you can frame your work through this lens, it really helps other people understand your value.

## Find your role by bridging gaps

Priorities usually shift in the post-deal environment, and the new vision will place a higher priority on a new set of goals. Make sure you're clear on the new vision so you understand what's important post deal. This will allow you to be strategic in applying the vision to your role and your team's role moving forward. Next, look for the gaps in knowledge, processes, or operations that you and/or your team can bridge. For example, if a top priority in the post-deal landscape is easing the transition for key clients, determine if there's anything you and your team can do differently to support this goal. You have line of sight on things that senior leadership doesn't. Leverage that knowledge to bridge those gaps. Even small things show that you're on board with the new vision, you understand why it's important, and you're part of the group of employees actively doing what the senior team thinks is most important.

## Take initiative

In the same vein as bridging gaps, you want to be proactive about your work. Look for ways to contribute to stalled projects. Especially those that align with your interests and support the new vision. Approach your boss, identify the opportunity, and ask if you can take the lead. A lot of times, things will sit until someone steps up. That's your opportunity to take a leadership role and contribute to the new direction—oftentimes even faster than you would have otherwise. This is a major opportunity for career advancement.

## Adapt your style to survive

New leaders will have new communication styles, priorities, and preferences. Your ability to get in good with these leaders will depend on how well you can adapt your own work style to meet theirs. You need to observe how they make decisions and what they prefer in terms of how people communicate or present to them. The onus is on you to figure out their preferences. This doesn't mean you should be inauthentic or compromise who you are (re-read the chapter on the Opportunist if you have forgotten why). It simply means being flexible and catering to the other person. Over the years, I've seen people who are shockingly good at this. Trust me, it's a skill that will take you places.

One special note for introverts who may struggle to adapt styles: you need to figure out how to let your new leaders know the value you bring and what you can contribute. They won't have the time or inclination to find that out. Again, it's on you to make sure they know.

With these strategies in mind, you'll be well-prepared to carve out your perfect niche at your growing company. But before we go any further, I recommend completing the following self-assessment to help analyze your current situation and decide what to do next. Take some time to truly reflect. Write down your answers so you can refer back to them in a few weeks, months, or even a year from now. This will help you check your progress and make sure you're still on the right path—or help you adjust your course as your goals change and your company evolves.

## Self-Assessment

### Where am I now?

1. Do I understand the vision and strategy of the new organization—the journey that we are on as a company with this post-deal news?

   - If yes, how does my role fit into the short/long term strategy of this new organization?

   - If no, how can I get smart on it and who can help me get there?

2. How do my values align with the new leadership and with the new company's vision, mission, and values?

3. How does my leadership team see my role with respect to the vision? Positively or negatively?

## Where do I want to be?

1.  Am I happy in my current role?

2.  How have my interests in future opportunities shifted post deal? Are there new roles, functions, or career paths I can see myself in?

3.  Is there a role I can create that can contribute to the new company vision? (This may take some time to discover.)

## How do I get there?

1.  What are ways I can position myself for future roles within the new organization?

2.  How will I go about acquiring the necessary skills and experiences needed? How can my leader(s) help me?

3.  What do I need to do to garner support for future roles?

This assessment is meant to help you see new opportunities to help carve out your perfect niche while adding value to your company. Just like any relationship, you're looking for a mutually good fit.

If you already see ways to leverage your skills, explore your interests, and contribute to the new vision, that's great! But if these things aren't immediately clear, give it some time. Chances are, your options will come into focus as you continue to work with new colleagues in the months ahead.

If several months go by and you still don't see how your interests and talents align with your company's new vision, it might be a sign that your job is no longer a good fit for you and it's time to move on. This can certainly happen. However, I want to point out that the vast majority of the time, there are many opportunities for people to help shape their role into something that's even more rewarding. The tricky part is navigating the post-deal environment to turn your aspirations into reality, when there are so many other leaders vying for the same kind of opportunities. That's what we'll cover next.

# CHAPTER 22

# Politics

If I failed to talk about politics, I'd be overlooking an inconvenient reality of the post-deal landscape. Unfortunately, things aren't always fair—both in the workplace and in life. And nowhere does that feel truer than in the post-deal landscape. It's all there: shifting alliances, betrayals, and unanticipated changes of heart. You can either choose to focus on the fact that this is a bummer (which it totally is) or you can decide right now to get past that because you're going to play this game to win. Make no mistake—I am not talking about clawing your way to the top. (Please *do not* claw your way to the top.) You need to accept the fact that perceptions, relationships, and image all matter in the workplace, and this is especially true during M&A.

On top of managing your personal brand, you're going to be surrounded by people who are scared, confused, and oftentimes appear to be losing their mind. This creates situations that feel like you are in a bad soap opera/horror movie/comedy. Yes, it can feel like all three at the same time.

Oh, the drama of M&A! My best advice is to stay out of the drama and gossip as much as you can. Assume the best intentions in others and do your best to remain dip-lomatic. Don't take sides—even when you really, really want to. Finger pointing hinders productive work, and it creates emotional reactions that make the workplace even less pleasant.

Taking the high road sounds easy in theory, but it can get a lot harder when you're working with people who don't hold themselves to similar standards. No matter how other people behave, *do not compromise your integrity*. The post-deal environment can make people feel incredibly insecure, and it creates the perfect storm for selfish, childish behav-ior. You'll see people doing anything they can to look good and save their own rear-ends. When this behavior comes from those you trust, it can feel like a kick to the gut. But don't stoop to their level and damage your own reputation. The short-term gains are not worth it, especially since the world is smaller than you think. Sometimes I think about post-deal dynamics like the TV show *Survivor*. Contestants will double-cross each other to make it to the next week on the show, but their slimy moves become forever engrained in their personal brand. People will remember how you treated them—both good and bad.

It's the politics that usually make M&A emotionally draining. Many people experience sadness, depression, stress, and anxiety in the months after a deal has been an-nounced. We touched on this in the Stages of Grief sec-tion, but it's important to recognize that politics can have an effect on your emotions as well. Studies on mind-body connection have shown that negative emotions can actu-ally make people feel physical soreness. So, if a person or situation at work has made you feel unappreciated, embarrassed, offended, or downright angry, it's important to realize that you're likely to carry those emotions with you and feel a physical impact as well.

The emotional drain of M&A is one of its worst side effects. It follows you out of the office and into your home. In researching this book, every interviewee, and I mean *every single one of them,* shared they had no idea how mentally, emotionally, and physically draining M&A deals can be. You're not the only one. Stay tuned to your psychological and physical well-being. Try to let things roll off your back as much as you can. It's natural that M&A can be tough, but it shouldn't be debilitating. If pain persists, take it seriously and consult a doctor or therapist. You need to be able to get past this so you can focus on taking positive actions that will help your career.

## Stronger together

After a deal, an employee's major focus should be enhancing visibility. *You need to be seen.* Otherwise, you can do great work and it can go unnoticed. This will not help you in reaching your goals—whatever they may be. But it is a fine line to walk when claiming credit for your work, and too much of it looks like you're bragging, showing off, or expecting recognition. This will quickly damage your reputation and likeability, especially with your newer colleagues.

A great way to navigate this hairy situation is by working together with your team. Recognition is key to your team's engagement, but it's also a great way to be visible without it coming across as self-serving. You are stronger together than you are alone, and as a group, you have a much greater power to lift each other up. Help your direct reports leverage their skills and talents, especially as it relates to the new vision. Their success is your success. And when your team members do great work, let your colleagues know! Look for opportunities to gain visibility as a team, and let your reports know that it's important for the team to look strong as a whole. Make it clear that this is a time to support one another—not cut each other down. Everyone should be using whatever mechanisms the company has in place to publicly recognize their team members. This sends a message to the rest of the company that your department is crushing it. There will be chaos throughout the organization, so if a team consistently seems highly functional, productive, and happy, that sends a strong message.

Another reason why team recognition is important is because it evens the playing field for introverts. This specific group of individuals tends to struggle the most with post-deal visibility. The loudest voices tend to crowd out others, and introverts can easily get lost in the shuffle— even if they are extremely talented. A few of the CEOs I interviewed brought up this problem as well, saying that it took them many years of M&A experience before they realized that high-potential introverts were routinely being overlooked. Be aware of this— whether you are an introvert or work with them. Raise the voice of introverts by highlighting the contributions they make to the team.

And if you're an introvert yourself, plan on stepping out of your comfort zone a bit to gain the visibility you need to thrive at the new organization. If you're reporting to a new boss, or if your boss' boss is new, actively reach out. Acknowledge that you might not be the loudest voice, but you are on board with the new mission and have valuable skills to contribute. That can go a long way to getting you noticed.

## Layoffs

Chances are very strong that the group of people you work with going into an M&A deal will be different than the group of people you work with a year later. As I explained in Section 1, one of the drivers of M&A is to gain efficiencies and reduce costs by eliminating redundancies at the newly formed organization. And it's almost a given that certain departments or positions will be over-staffed after a deal goes through, particularly in larger deals. Once the integration is set in motion, there won't be a need for two accounting departments, two marketing departments, or multiple sales reps for every territory. Here's where the politics really start to play out—good and bad.

Some people will pivot into new roles, but others will quit or be let go. Remember I shared at the beginning: the post-deal landscape is like a game of musical chairs. Not everyone will have a chair when the music stops, and getting a chair is not always contingent on your expertise. You should emotionally prepare yourself for this. It's a big change to go from seeing the same people five days a week over the course of many years to no longer seeing them at all. It can be incredibly sad. And it's even harder if you feel like good people were let go when they should have kept their jobs. But no matter how upset or angry you are, it doesn't serve anyone to vent at work or let your bitterness show. It won't get anyone's job back, and you don't want it to keep you from doing your own job. I'm not saying don't get angry. You can scream, cry, throw things, and go on about the injustice of it all, but save all of that until you leave the office. Equally important, don't involve your colleagues in your emotional reactions—even outside of the office. You want to be known for your steadiness and what you can contribute, not for emotional outbursts. Just like navigating the stages of M&A grief, you need to get from denial to acceptance when it comes to layoffs.

Companies run on people. And people aren't perfect. As you continue navigating the post-deal environment, processing the changes around you, remember that companies are made up of imperfect people. We're not always logical. We're emotional. We can be impulsive on the one hand and slow to make decisions on the other. And it's hard for us to process change. You will witness a lot of imperfect behavior post deal. It's important to keep this in mind when things get hard—no, *especially* when things get hard. As individuals and as employees, we're stronger together than we are alone, even with our imperfections.

CHAPTER 23

# Thriving

Have you ever noticed that when you're going someplace you've never been, the journey to get there seems to take much longer than the trip back? When you don't know where you're headed, your mind is on full alert, analyzing your surroundings and trying to make sense of everything. The effort of constantly trying to get your bearings makes time slow down, and your trip becomes labor-intensive. But on the way home, and on future trips to the same place, the journey seems to go much quicker because you can relax and get into your groove. You know what to expect, and you know you can handle all of the turns in the road, so you don't stress.

In writing this book, my goal was to familiarize you with the M&A journey, so it doesn't feel like you're on an unknown path. Whether you're going through your first M&A or you've been through several, it's incredibly helpful to build your awareness of the post-deal landscape so you know what to expect. This will make you feel more comfortable, more confident, and better able to continue doing your best work.

With that in mind, here are some final tips to help you thrive through an M&A deal.

- **Always know what skillsets are most valuable and marketable.** This will help you be strategic about the new skillsets you choose to go after in the future. You want these skills to help you at this job, and for years to come—wherever you may go. Staying on top of industry trends and new technologies is a given. We all need to keep learning and upskilling, even when it seems like we're too busy to focus on anything outside of what's required.

- **Be a solutions-based person.** Instead of complaining about problems or thinking you can't make a difference, try to be a problem-solver. A simple shift in mindset can make a huge difference. And there truly are many more things in your control than you realize.

- **Make sure your new colleagues understand the role you play and why it's valuable.** Don't be obstinate, but don't assume they know what you do. Over time, newly formed companies often come to see the value of roles they had initially underestimated. This comes from gaining a greater understanding of the roles, the acquired company, and the industry. To make this move faster, be proactive.

- **Be patient with your colleagues—even if they resemble the cast of characters in this book.** Fear brings out the worst in people. Remember that the behaviors you see in the workplace are temporary. People take on personas to help themselves survive, and this more or less goes back to normal with time. Chances are, you can see elements of yourself in some or all of the characters in this book. Before you go pointing fingers at others, take a hard look at yourself. Try to be the best version of yourself even when times are tough and your colleagues are more likely to follow suit,

- **Build your resilience.** When you're frustrated, try to gain perspective. Five years from now, will you remember how your coworker messed up a report or went behind your back? Probably not. Think long term. Life is a marathon not a sprint. And since life is an endurance sport, you need to have the energy to keep going. Don't waste emotional energy on things that aren't worth it. Millions of people have gone through M&A. Just like them, you will survive.

- **Acknowledge the end of the old way to start anew.** As William Bridges, the father of surviving corporate transition said, "transition begins with an ending and finishes with a beginning."[40] By acknowledging the end of the old way, mentally or (even better) through some type of ceremony, you can refresh your perspective and start anew with heightened effectiveness. But to really capitalize on these opportunities, you must acknowledge that things have changed. Recognize the M&A as an informative milestone in your life, even if you have mixed feelings.

- **Find effective ways to manage your stress.** Mindfulness has come into vogue lately because it works. Whether you take up a weekly yoga practice or you use an app like Headspace for guided meditation, find something that makes you release your worries and anxieties. It sounds straightforward, but self-care is one of the first things to go out the window when we get busy and overwhelmed, and this can impact our physical health. Don't let this happen. And don't obsess over things that are not in your control. You can waste a lot of time worrying about something over which you can do nothing. Save your energy for things that matter.

- **Remember that the grass always looks greener on the other side—even when it isn't.** Don't jump at the first opportunity for a job at another company. You have equity with your current company, and you will have to build up equity all over again if you go somewhere else. Aside from that uphill battle, no company is perfect. Even if your future doesn't look like what you had initially hoped, you never know how things will pan out. Don't give up, because things can always change. Be patient, have the right attitude, and give yourself the best chance at success.

Lastly, with all of the emotional turmoil of M&A, it's easy to focus only on yourself. (What can you do to get that promotion? How will you get noticed? What project will get you in front of the right leaders?) We talk a lot about that kind of thing in this book, but I want to make sure you know that truly thriving in M&A is about more than that.

When I work with teams going through M&A, I always talk about rediscovering the humanity in business. When it comes down to it, people are often overlooked in M&A decisions, even though they are what make businesses run. And when people are overlooked, they feel like they have to look out for themselves. This can create an ugly shift from a team-based culture to a me-first, every-man-for-himself culture. When you're aware of this risk, it becomes easier to be part of the solution rather than part of the problem.

Do your best to be a role model for positive behavior. Demonstrate integrity, class, and grace. And when you successfully make that transition from denial to acceptance, help others get there too. This is how you will become a better leader and the best version of yourself.

# About the Author

Jennifer J Fondrevay is the Founder of Day1 Ready™, a consultancy that advises forward-thinking business leaders, owners and C-Suite executives on how to prepare for the human capital challenges of M&A. As a Fortune 500 C-Suite "survivor" of three multibillion-dollar acquisitions, Jennifer has been on all sides of the deal equation. She has seen countless growth strategies fail due to a workforce that couldn't pivot and adapt as quickly as leadership anticipated.

She shares her expertise as broadly as she can and has contributed to: Harvard Business Review, Thrive Global, American Marketing Association and Middle Market Growth; and has been a frequent podcast guest and keynote speaker for HR conferences, associations and Fortune 500 companies.

Jennifer holds a dual BA degree in Political Science and French from the University of Illinois at Urbana-Champaign, and a Masters in International Management from the Thunderbird School of Global Management (a.k.a Thunderbird), coincidentally acquired by Arizona State University in 2014.

# Acknowledgements

How can you possibly be expected to fit on two pages all of the people you need to thank and honor regarding your book? This book drew from a collection of my personal and professional experiences over a lifetime. That's a lot of people who contributed to me and the thinking that would result in this book. Here goes anyway.

To my mother and father who instilled a strong sense of justice and clear values in me from an early age. Always do the right thing was deeply embedded in me. Add to that, their belief that I must have passion for whatever I did, give credit when it is due and articulate my thoughts clearly if I ever hoped to lead people. With all of that coaching early on, it is likely of little shock to people who knew my parents and me growing up that I would write this type of book. And they believed in this crazy book idea from the very beginning. Thanks Pops and Abuelita.

For my husband Greg and my children, Yvonne and Connor, thank you for your love, patience, support, back tickles, foot rubs, picking up after yourselves, walking the dog more often, and letting me sleep in whenever possible. How could I have ever done this without you all as my solid foundation? Thanks in particular to my kids for not getting in trouble with the law while mom was distracted writing a book.

Consider this one big group hug to the many clubs, associations, organizations and FB communities of which I have been a part which include some of the kindest, sharpest, most selfless people I know. When you work in corporate for 25 years, you tend to get a bit jaded and think everyone has a hidden agenda. I left corporate to write this book and these groups each restored my faith in humanity and for some odd reason, they all believed in me without being compensated. They include (in no particular order because I love 'em all): Dorie Clark and her Recognized Expert Facebook community, filled with people who are a reminder that being successful and nice are not mutually exclusive; Dorothy Carlson, the Glenview Tennis Club and all players and coaches who reminded me what great teamwork (and winning) can do for your spirits; the Association for Corporate Growth, especially the women in the Corporate office and Detroit chapter, who believed in my message and promoted it in every way you could, including podcast, interviews, articles, presentations and panels, (you ladies went above and beyond); to the DisruptHR and Ignite communities in Chicago and beyond who loved my message and encouraged me to get it out there (so long as I did it in 5 minutes); Jeffrey Hayzlett's C-Suite Advisors and Thought Council, thank you for cheering me on through some personal setbacks; EDGE Women Speakers, I couldn't ask for a greater group of women with whom to share the microphone; and finally to the Million Dollar Posse and the Windy City Professional Speakers, my tribe of speaking powerhouses who continually push me to up my game.

And now for the people who actively contributed to the development of this book, either in interviews, writing guidance, book development and production, or just general pep talks when I needed them most. This book truly would not exist without you. When it comes to the writing, there are so many people to thank whom I cannot name. My interviews were "off-the-record" to allow people to share their unvarnished experiences, so I am offering one big broad thank you to my interviewees who contributed their precious time and insights to make this book a valuable and truthful playbook.

To Amelia Forczak, you have been my partner in crime throughout this book journey, from writing through production. You and the pithywordsmithery.com team helped make sure the birth of this book stayed true to my original vision AND made it better. To Danny Schuman, my book publisher yoda and to Jess Hanebury, you're the funniest graphic designer I've had the pleasure to collaborate with, which stands out as much as your talent. To the amazingly talented Jeff York, the wrist behind each of my fabulous illustrations. You were with me from the beginning and made such invaluable contributions beyond the incredible caricatures. To every person who provided a testimonial for my book, both in my front pages, website and on Amazon, I am indebted. Finally to Mark Bonchek and Ron Carucci, who were conversations #1 and #2 when I first contemplated going down this path. I don't know whether to thank you or curse you.

Finally, included within this list are all of the individuals who played an influential role in helping me get to this point. You each helped me, whether mentally, spiritually or physically, to believe in what I was doing early on and especially now. My undying gratitude to each of you: Andrew Williams, Anne Martino, Barry Goodman, Beth Killion, Betsi Roach, Caroline Molina-Ray, Caroline Stokes, Carrie Lannon, Christina Martini, Christy Long-Hoskins, Dana Todd, Dave Mullen, Dean Petrulakis, Deb Dietz, Debbie Vyskocil, Doug Robbins, Erin O'Malley, Jacqueline Baptist, Jason Tuzinkewich, Jeanette Bronee, Jennifer Kraus, Jennifer Masi, John Bravo, John Glavin, John Stap, Kathleen Overholt, Kelly Smith, Kim Caviness, Kim Feil, Lauren Vickers, Lisa Hunt, Mary Beth Ellis, Marty Stock, Mia McNary, Michele Herbst, Michelle Henriksen, Michelle Janowski, Natasha Todorovic, Paige Boyd, Peter Switzer, Ralph Dieckmann, Renuka Sastri, Robbie Samuels, Robert Snyder, Steven Handmaker, Sandi Digras, Tom Marquardt, Tom Stewart, Tracy Garden.

It takes a village. To anyone who feels I didn't acknowledge him or her properly, hit me up and I'll buy you a drink.

# Pass it On

If you have enjoyed this book, please pass it on to someone you know who could use it. Or buy them the book!

Experiencing a merger or an acquisition can be traumatizing if you don't know what to expect. My goal is to help as many people as possible to navigate the murky waters to see the opportunities.

Thanks for passing it on. And feel free to leave an Amazon review.

# References

1   Jennifer Fondrevay, "After a Merger, Don't Let 'Us vs. Them' Thinking Ruin the Company," *Harvard Business Review*, May 21, 2018. https://hbr.org/2018/05/after-a-merger-dont-let-us-vs-them-thinking-ruin-the-company

2   "The Big Idea: The New M&A Playbook," by Clayton Chrisensen, Richard Alton, Curtis Rising and Andrew Waldeck. *Harvard Business Review*, March 2011 issue

3   Roger L. Martin, "M&A: The One Thing You Need to Get Right," *Harvard Business Review*, June 2016. https://hbr.org/2016/06/ma-the-one-thing-you-need-to-get-right

4   Shahram Heshmat Ph.D, "What Is Loss Aversion?" *Psychology Today*, March 8, 2018. https://www.psychologytoday.com/us/blog/science-choice/201803/what-is-loss-aversion

5   Amos Tversky and Daniel Kahneman, "Advances in prospect theory: Cumulative representation of uncertainty," *Journal of Risk and Uncertainty*, 5 (4) (1992): 297–323.

6   vi. "British Empire," *Wikipedia*. https://en.wikipedia.org/wiki/British_Empire

7   Emmanuel Mensah and Joseph Mensah Onumah, *Mergers and Acquisitions in the Era of Globalization: The Ghanian Experience*. http://www.na-businesspress.com/JAF/MensahE_Web17_3_.pdf

8   Anastasia, "A Historical Analysis of M&A Waves," *Cleverism*, January 26, 2016. https://www.cleverism.com/historical-analysis-ma-waves-mergers-acquisition/

9   "List of Largest Mergers and Acquisitions," *Wikipedia*. https://en.wikipedia.org/wiki/List_of_largest_mergers_and_acquisitions

10   "How Technology Is Changing M&A in the U.S.," *Harvard Business Review*, May 18, 2018. https://hbr.org /sponsored/2018/05/how-technology-is-changing-ma-in-the-u-s

11   Constance L. Hays, "Ben & Jerry's To Unilever, With Attitude," *New York Times*, April 13, 2000. https://www.nytimes. com/2000/04/13/business/ben-jerry-s-to-unilever-with-attitude.html

12   Evelyn M. Rusli, "Facebook Buys Instagram for $1 Billion," *DealBook*, *New York Times*, April 9, 2012. https://dealbook. nytimes.com/2012/04/09/facebook-buys-instagram-for-1-billion/

13   Robert Greene, *The 48 Laws of Power* (London: Penguin, 2000).

14   Elizabeth Kübler-Ross, *On Death and Dying* (London: Tavistock, 1973).

15   William Bidges and Susan Bridges, *Managing Transitions* (Da Capo Lifelong Books, 2017).
     Chip Heath and Dan Heath, *The Power of Moments* (London: Corgi, 2019).

16   Claes Janssen, a Swedish social psychologist, helped define the stages of change as a four-roomed apartment: with rooms of contentment, denial, confusion and renewal. He believed that once a person was prepared to move out of denial, their first task was to help others to come to the same realization.

17   Author of *Surviving Corporate Transition* I mentioned before who saved my life. The father of transition management, he built on Kübler-Ross's stages of grief and expanded on them by describing the stages of transition in a corporate setting. After you read this book, I encourage you to read his book *Managing Transitions, Making the Most of Change...* but not until I've helped you as much as possible with this book!

18   Kübler-Ross, *On Death and Dying*, p. 100

19    Kayla Matthews, "The Value of Learning to Read
      Between the Lines in Business," *Successful Blog*,
      July 13, 2017. https://www.successful-blog.com/1/
      value-learning-read-between-the-lines-business/

20    Richard Branson, "Richard Branson Explains How to
      Master the Art of Reading Between the Lines," *Business
      Insider*, October 29, 2015. https://www.businessinsider.com/
      richard-branson-how-to-be-an-effective-listener-2015-10

21    F. Diane Barth, "What's the Best Way to Handle a Know-
      It-All?" *Psychology Today*, December 21, 2013. https://
      www.psychologytoday.com/us/blog/the-couch/201312/
      what-s-the-best-way-handle-know-it-all

22    Jacqueline Smith, "8 Tips For Dealing With a Know-It-All
      Coworker," *Forbes*, September 9, 2013. https://www.forbes.com/
      sites/jacquelynsmith/2013/09/09/8-tips-for-dealing-with-a-
      know-it-all-coworker/#40a1ae953853

23    "Employee Tenure in 2018," *BLS*, September 20, 2018. https://
      www.bls.gov/news.release/pdf/tenure.pdf. The median number
      of years that wage and salary workers had been with their
      current employer in a 2018 survey by the U.S. Bureau of Labor
      Statistics was 4.2 years. Generally, median employee tenure was
      higher among older workers than younger ones.

24    Robert Greene, *The 48 Laws of Power* (London: Penguin, 2000).

25    "Missing in action," *Merriam-Webster*. https://www.merriam-
      webster.com/dictionary/missing%20in%20action "Missing and
      unable to be confirmed as captured or killed following military
      action."

26    Jim Harter, "Employee Engagement on the Rise in the U.S.,"
      *Gallup*, August 26, 2018. https://news.gallup.com/poll/241649/
      employee-engagement-rise.aspx

27    Marc Miller, "Are You a Generalist or Specialist and Why
      It Makes a Difference," *Career Pivot*. https://careerpivot.
      com/2018/are-you-a-generalist-or-specialist/

28  Caroline Ceniza-Levine, "To Advance in Your Career,
    Is It Better To Be a Specialist or Generalist?" *Forbes*,
    January 30, 2018. https://www.forbes.com/sites/
    carolinecenizalevine/2018/01/30/to-advance-in-your-career-is-
    it-better-to-be-a-specialist-or-generalist/#31e37d02493e

29  "What is William Bridges' Transition Model?" *William Bridges
    Associates*. https://wmbridges.com/what-is-transition/

30  Ithai Stern and James D. Westphal, "Stealthy Footsteps to
    the Boardroom: Executives' Backgrounds, Sophisticated
    Interpersonal Influence Behavior, and Board Appointments,"
    *Administrative Science* Quarterly, 55 (2) (2010): 278–319.
    "As part of a study, Stern and his co-author James Westphal,
    strategy professor at the University of Michigan's Ross School
    of Business, drew from theory and research on interpersonal
    attraction, as well as interviews with 42 managers and CEOs
    of large U.S. industrial and service firms, to identify a set of
    tactics that are less likely to be interpreted as manipulative or
    political in intent, and are therefore more likely to bring about
    social influence. The researchers identified seven effective
    forms of ingratiation most likely to help executives win board
    seats." Aaron Mays writing in "Flattery Will Get You Far,"
    *Kellogg News & Events*, August 16, 2010. https://www.kellogg.
    northwestern.edu/news_articles/2010/ithai-stern.aspx

31  "The Meaning and Origin of the Expression: Bury Your Head
    in the Sand," *The Phrase Finder*. https://www.phrases.org.uk/
    meanings/bury-your-head-in-the-sand.html
    "The story was first recorded by the Roman writer Pliny
    the Elder, who suggested that ostriches hide their heads in
    bushes. Ostriches don't hide, either in bushes or sand, although
    they do sometimes lie on the ground to make themselves
    inconspicuous. The 'burying their head in the sand' myth is
    likely to have originated from people observing them lowering
    their heads when feeding." (This myth has been debunked but
    for the purposes of our Ostrich character description let's roll
    with it.)

32  "Denial: When It Helps, When It Hurts," *Mayo Clinic*. https://
    www.mayoclinic.org/healthy-lifestyle/adult-health/in-depth/
    denial/art-20047926

33  "Denial," *Mayo Clinic*.

34   Linda Bartman, *Navigating & Managing Your Brand in an era of Mergers and Acquisitions panel for AMA*, November 2018.

35   Dale Carnegie, *How to Win Friends and Influence People* (New York: Gallery, 1998).

36   Jodi Navta, *Navigating & Managing Your Brand in an era of Mergers and Acquisitions panel for AMA*, November 2018.

37   Brett Harned, "How to Clear Project Confusion with a RACI Chart," *TeamGantt*, August 13, 2018. https://www.teamgantt.com/blog/raci-chart-definition-tips-and-example

38   Fondrevay, "After a Merger, Don't Let 'Us vs. Them' Thinking Ruin the Company"

39   "Accomplishment Statements Guide," *Winthrop University Career and Civic Engagement*. https://www.winthrop.edu/uploadedFiles/cce/AccomplishmentStatementHandout.pdf

40   William Bidges and Susan Bridges, *Managing Transitions* (Da Capo Lifelong Books, 2017).